H-UNIT

H-UNIT

A STORY OF WRITING AND

REDEMPTION BEHIND THE

WALLS OF SAN QUENTIN

Keith and Kent Zimmerman

TURNER
PUBLISHING COMPANY

TURNER PUBLISHING COMPANY

200 4th Avenue North • Suite 950
Nashville, Tennessee 37219

445 Park Avenue • 9th Floor
New York, NY 10022

www.turnerpublishing.com

H-Unit: A Story of Writing and Redemption Behind the Walls of San Quentin

Note: All inmate names appearing in this work have been changed, and the writing passages within are author renderings of the kind of prose done in class.

Cover design by Gina Binkley
Book design by Glen Edelstein
Cover image copyright © 2012 Ashley Crary

Library of Congress Cataloging-in-Publication Data

Zimmerman, Keith.
H-unit : A story of writing and redemption behind the walls of San Quentin / Keith & Kent Zimmerman.
  p. cm.
ISBN 978-1-68162-936-0
1. Prisoners--Education--California--San Quentin. 2. Prisoners--Services for--California--San Quentin. 3. Arts in prison--California--San Quentin. 4. Prisoners as authors--California--San Quentin. 5. Prisoners' writings, American. 6. Zimmerman, Keith. 7. Zimmerman, Kent. 8. California State Prison at San Quentin. I. Zimmerman, Kent. II. Title.
HV8883.3.U52S268 2012
365'.666--dc23
 2012014186

Printed in the United States of America
12 13 14 15 16 17 18—0 9 8 7 6 5 4 3 2 1

The Zimmermen dedicate their work on this book
to Doris and Joe.
Love,
Keith and Kent

Acknowledgments

The following people have inspired us and mattered throughout this project: Doris Zimmerman, Gladys Zimmerman, Deborah Zimmerman, Laura Bowman-Salzsieder, Jill Brown, Ashley Crary, Ken Druckerman, Adam Amdur, Todd Bottorff, Diane Gedymin, Christina Huffines, Ann Moller, Steve Ross, Joe Rose, William Watson, Robert McCrary, van Löben Sels/RembeRock Foundation, Mike Ness, Shane Trulin, Steven Rybicki, Bill Hillmann, Brian Murphy, Dinero D the Dynamic "P," Nitin Abraham, Scott Budnick, the CO's at SQSP who watch over us, Ed Preciado, Michael Tolkin, Anne Marino, Gladys Phillips, Philip Bailey, David Mairs, Jordan Harari, Alan Black, Erica Linderholm, Jack Boulware, Naveen and Vin Abraham, Tim Pitt Gordon, Tim Dufore, Jane Ganahl, _The Class_ (book and movie) by François Bégaudeau, Gregory Carter, Kevin Whiteley, Sandra & Art Rybicki, Paul McNabb, Rolf Kissman, Richard Walsh, Frank Calabrese, Jr., and the mindful men at H-Unit—past, present and future—who "program" for a better tomorrow.

Contents

H-UNIT

PROLOGUE

Collaborators to the Incorrigibles

For as long as we remember being in California, starting in the summer of 1963 before the November assassination of John F. Kennedy, San Quentin has been a phantom force that lurked in the shadows of our childhoods. We were ten years old when Joe and Doris Zimmerman, our East Coast working-class parents, pulled up stakes in East McKeesport, Pennsylvania (the birthplace and home of Andy Warhol) and headed west to the Promised Land in Northern California. "The Twins"—that's us, identical, born twenty minutes apart—were about to experience our first major seismic shift in life.

"Kids, we're going on vacation to California," Joe announced over supper with one curious caveat, "but don't tell any of your friends. We might not be coming back."

With $2,500 of borrowed cash and a refurbished 1955 Chevy station wagon with a fresh coat of Earl Sheib baby blue paint, and with my father and mother sharing equal turns behind the wheel, we rumbled and sputtered across the United States in search of a new America.

Once we crossed the California border, and settled in Sonoma County—specifically Santa Rosa, a stone's throw from the lush Napa Valley wine country—Joe found a "dream job" as a wholesaler for a floor covering and carpeting distributor. Being a salesman on the road meant frequent trips servicing retail stores from Marin County all the way north to the Oregon border. There were lots of weekend day trips to visit aunts and uncles already living in Marin County and the East Bay, which meant frequent jaunts across the Richmond San Rafael Bridge. Whenever we crossed that bridge, our father would announce the presence of San Quentin State Prison. ("I'm gonna drop you kids off there if you don't behave.") It was the first Marin County landmark to greet northbound drivers who exited the bridge on their way back through middling towns like San Rafael, Novato, Petaluma, and then home to Santa Rosa, once dubbed by horticulturist Luther Burbank as "the city designed for living."

Since our very first time driving past its walls, San Quentin State Prison has had the same gold amber beige paint job it dons today, and its arched portals and towers remain visible through the frequent fog. The prison stands next to and is named after the small bayside hamlet nestled in unincorporated Marin County.

Joe's first trip inside the walls of San Quentin was strictly business. He was there to inspect and replace some defective linoleum that had been installed by one of the stores carrying his product line. The sight of San Quentin inmates as "regular Joes" had a huge and instantaneous affect on him. San Quentin State Prison mesmerized Joe. Over the dinner table, he described its thick limestone walls, the multitiered cell blocks, the gigantic mess hall murals, but mainly the men. He marveled to our family how the inmates—white, black, whatever—were no different than him. Very few of them seemed like the monsters he'd expected from watching George Raft movies. As a result, he had an idea. He would explore the possibility of volunteering at San Quentin, teaching salesmanship, a skill any red-blooded parolee could use to earn himself an honest living upon release. Ultimately Joe's dream died on the vine. Whether he failed to penetrate the bureaucracy, who knew?

In lieu of Joe's unsuccessful attempt to pursue his dream at the prison, the aura of San Quentin later manifested itself in a more artistic light. In February 1969, we purchased a copy of *Johnny Cash at San Quentin* the week it was released. The image of a stately silhouetted Johnny at San Quentin bathed in blue light represented common ground between our father and us. Our entire family soon became Cash fans as Johnny snarled, "San Quentin, I hate every inch of you." Cash vinyl got double duty; played loud while the folks were away, played soft after dinner when everyone was together under one roof. The boom-chucka, boom-chucka of Bob Dylan's "Wanted Man," the hopeful gospel harmonies of "Peace in the Valley," but mainly the dual title tracks, both versions of "San Quentin," fit snugly into our family's groove.

Johnny Cash carried huge weight in our clan. He wasn't a longhair, though his hair was thick and swept back past his collar. He loved America, but he had a rebellious streak where he couldn't be spoon fed blind patriotism. Although he had his publicized problems with pills, he didn't glorify drug use. In a Cash song, the cops weren't always the good guys. Outlaws were cool. Native Americans held dignity. He was the singer who wore black "for the poor and beaten down." He did so also for the prisoner, a victim of the times, who paid for his transgressions. He discovered, as we would, that it's possible to simultaneously love and hate a place like a century-and-a-half old prison. "San-Quentin-I-hate-every-inch-of-you" would soon become words to live by.

Fast forward to 2000. By the turn of the twenty-first century our writing careers were in full swing. We had spent over two decades in the music business as journalists and editors for a weekly music industry trade magazine called *Gavin*. Our two-plus decades in the music business were a rich and accomplished segment of our lives. We crossed paths personally and journalistically with many of our heroes growing up; a myriad of songwriters and artists like Bob Dylan, George Harrison, Paul McCartney, Lou Reed, Willie Nelson, Kris Kristofferson, Emmy Lou Harris, Bruce Springsteen, Leonard Cohen, Chrissie Hynde, R.E.M., and the list goes on and on. Through our writings at *Gavin,* we met John Lydon, aka Johnny Rotten of the Sex Pistols and became the co-authors of Lydon's 1994 hit autobiography, *Rotten: No Irish, No Blacks, No Dogs.*

Writing *Rotten* with John Lydon opened new doors toward working with a whole crew of "bad asses" and malcontents. Before we started John's book, the mere mention of the Sex Pistols would launch Lydon into a tirade. The past was a sticking point with John, who is obsessed with the here and now. John is and will always be a man who marches to his own drummer. We love and admire him deeply.

Rotten hit the Top Five in the *London Times* and Number One on the *Evening Standard* book list, and has been published in several languages. After working with Lydon and living to talk about it, we became known in publishing circles as Collaborators to the Incorrigibles.

In 2000, *Hell's Angel: The Life and Times of Sonny Barger and the Hell's Angels Motorcycle Club* became our first co-authored *New York Times* bestseller. The morning the book made the *Times* list, Jim Fitzgerald, our editor-turned-literary-agent, called us on the phone. "This is a big thing for you. Life will change," he warned us. And it did change us, only in ways we didn't anticipate.

With the success of *Hell's Angel* and *Rotten,* we found ourselves standing at the crossroads. Just as we had anticipated, as the twenty-first century approached, the music business infrastructure had crumbled rapidly as a result of the industry's widespread mistrust of change and new technology. Major labels and music radio across the United States, instead of adjusting to the times, conglomerized further, merged tighter, and litigated often. As a result, there was no sense remaining in the music business. So we departed with our reputations intact.

What to do now?

Naturally, we decided to immerse ourselves into the publishing world as full-time authors. As an ambitious two-man, hired gun writing team, our output would quickly swell to over a dozen book projects. Looking back, we didn't realize how volatile it was being full-time authors, living off advances, royalties, and ancillary rights. In addition, after a lifetime of "take" and being self-absorbed with career matters, it was also time for us to "give back," simple as that. The question remained, what to do? And, specifically, how and what can we give back?

For us, it started one afternoon in 2002 when Kent visited an old college professor he hadn't seen in decades. Dr. Stuart Hyde was an inspirational teacher, an excellent professor and former chairman of the Broadcast Arts Department at San Francisco State University. Kent's re-acquaintance with Dr. Hyde would prove decisive. He told Stuart of our intentions to write a few more books and then grab an MFA creative writing degree and perhaps move on to academia and teaching, preferably at a college or university.

At the time, we were about to embark on our next book with Sonny Barger for William Morrow. Dr. Hyde confessed that he had worked with offenders and found his most fulfilling teaching experience not at San Francisco State University, but, of all places, behind the walls of San Quentin where he taught broadcasting for eleven years. Dr. Hyde's face lit up as he recalled his experiences teaching the inmates, and how "people are people," and without the prison trappings, how hard it would be to differentiate his students from Normal Joes on the bus.

Kent immediately flashed on our father Joe's identical observation. It was then that our teaching mission radically changed, or, rather, expanded. Get the piece of MFA paper, chase a teaching position, but in the interim months, gain valuable teaching experience at San Quentin. This new plan had the essences of writing a good book: danger, uncertainty, challenge, and doing something outside of our comfort zones. Where do we sign up?

Dr. Hyde retired to his kitchen, dialed the telephone and made a call. He came back out and handed Kent a torn slip of paper. Written on it was a name and phone number: Jean Bracy, San Quentin State Prison. A couple weeks later we mailed a letter that marked the beginning of a whole new adventure.

11/05/2002
Jean Bracy
Education Department
San Quentin State Prison
San Quentin, CA 94964

Dear Jean:

We spoke recently on the telephone regarding our interest in teaching a creative writing course for the San Quentin Education Department. As promised, here is some information.

As twin brothers, we are a writing team headquartered in Oakland, having published a wide range of books in the space of the last ten years, including popular culture, music, and art. After having spent twenty-plus years in the music business, both in publishing a weekly music trade magazine as well as two years in high tech, we became full time writers in August of 2001. We're scheduled to begin a Masters of Fine Arts program in Creative Writing in 2003.

Our output has resulted in bestsellers here and abroad, both on the *New York Times* Bestseller list and on international lists. We've written in the autobiography, nonfiction, short story, and fiction genres for major publishing houses.

That said, we're most noted as the writers behind Ralph "Sonny" Barger's two recent bestsellers, *Hell's Angel: The Life and Times of Sonny Barger* and *Ridin' High, Livin' Free*, a book of motorcycle short stories. *Hell's Angel* is currently translated in 14 languages. Just last week we turned in a novel, an action thriller to be published in 2003.

We're assuming that our association with Mr. Barger could be an issue. We see it as an extreme positive as far as relating to the men. It was after graduating from the education system at Folsom Prison that influenced Sonny to become a reader and an author.

Of course, we would submit to any necessary background checks. As far as classroom curriculum, it could be as wide as necessary, best summed up as "finding your voice and getting it onto the page." Anything from writing letters to short stories, novels, memoirs, and autobiographies, even a bit of poetry would be fair game. Examples of great writing would be presented. But mainly the course would revolve around the submissions and discussions of student work. Our teaching experience includes hosting hundreds of seminars and guest teaching and lecturing on the university level.

We sincerely feel that we have something unique to offer and would appreciate having the opportunity to discuss this further in person. We'll be in touch soon.

Sincerely,

Kent & Keith Zimmerman

CHAPTER 1

Blues for Bobby

Bobby Lee was the first student in our class to die.

Bobby Lee's face belied his 48 years. Short in stature, African American, well-liked, this was the kind of guy of whom a person would ask, "What is this guy doing locked up?" He may have been a streetwise criminal (the *San Jose Mercury News* reported that Bobby had been involved in burglaries, drug possession and an assault case), but he didn't seem the violent, aggressive, in-your-face type. But in a classroom environment, who does?

Bobby regularly sat in the far corner, right next to the door of H-Unit's Education Classroom. He was bespectacled, erudite looking, and soft spoken. The "ReadBacks" were his favorite part of the class. He liked to participate in the writing assignments; other times he enjoyed just listening to the other class members' writings being read back. His attendance was so consistent that after a two-week absence, we began to wonder,

"Where's Bobby?"

One day in 2005, Bobby Lee was diagnosed with bronchitis, or possibly pneumonia. After he was prescribed some over-the-counter drugs like cough syrup, Tylenol, and Benadryl, along with a fistful of antibiotics, Bobby collapsed on his way back to his H-Unit bunk. A day later, he was rushed to nearby Marin General Hospital where his heart stopped three times en route to hospital care. He died in Marin General due to massive bleeding into his lungs. Soon after his death, the H-Unit gossip mill was abuzz with whispers that Bobby's ambulance ride out of San Quentin was needlessly delayed. One preposterous story had the ambulance driver stopping for a snack on the way to the hospital. (One of the first things we learned about prison yards like H-Unit is that they make office water cooler gossip mills look like a G3 Summit.)

A few days after Bobby's death, we attended a memorial service held up on "the Hill," in the Protestant chapel on San Quentin's North Block, overlooking the picture postcard San Francisco Bay view. North Block and the Hill—the main areas of the prison—are where the Death Row inmates and the "lifers" are housed, men condemned or serving decades for serious violent and anti-social crimes such as murder, armed robbery, and drug dealing.

We drove across the Richmond San Rafael Bridge to pay final tribute to Bobby. Turns out it was a two-for-one funeral service staged inside San Quentin's walls. Another Latino inmate who had died of cancer was also being memorialized. At the front of the chapel near the pulpit was a color photocopy of Bobby's prison ID picture scotch-taped to a music stand. (Inmates look ominous on their prison ID cards, partly because some photos are taken after a days-long, milk-cart-run bus journey on the infamous "Gray Goose," which drops off and picks up inmates from several county jails or state institutions on the way to SQ.)

Without his glasses, Bobby's picture lacked the more studious features we remembered him by. On the one-page memorial handout, his last name was misspelled. Seated on the chapel's pews were four dozen or so black and Latin inmates. We were among a handful of whites attending the service.

The minister delivered a religious eulogy for Bobby and the other fallen Latin inmate. After a couple of hymns, prayers, and

Bible passages, members of the audience were invited to come up and speak about the recently departed. When it looked as if nobody would venture a public pronouncement on Bobby's behalf, we looked at each other. Then Kent walked slowly to the front of the chapel, unfolding a couple of sheets of paper from his back pocket—a print-out of the words that Bobby had written in class.

Bobby's kinetic prose came alive. Short, powerful, street-smart bursts of narrative. And suddenly the man whose sullen image was taped to the music stand rose like Lazarus across the room with colorful and vibrant tales and anecdotes of his locked down routine. The first piece was a sardonic, comedic account of two men having to share a six-by-five-foot patch of dorm, upper and lower housing bunks, two small lockers with feet dangling over their bunks. The second passage detailed a painful, gut-wrenching breakup with a woman on the driveway of Bobby's Oakland pad. The third piece was a lighthearted account of Bobby Lee the Player hitting a local East 14th Street Oaktown nightclub on the weekend, having some fun before Stormy Monday came around.

Bobby's fourth and final offering was the *piece de resistance:* a declarative call to battle on the mean streets of East Oakland. It resonated with a rousing tone reminiscent of Henry V's Shakespearean St. Crispin's Day speech the night before the 1415 battle of Agincourt.

> Gather up the mob. It's time to take another turf and a high price lawyer to stand and defend ya! There's another funeral to attend. Mama just received the news that her son is dead in the ghettos of Oakland, California. City of Ballers and Jackers is where I'm from! As we roll through the 'hoods, getting money ain't no joke as we slide through Bushrod in the north, Acorns, Ghost Town, Funk Town, High Street, Seminary, 69 Village, 98th Avenue, Brookfield, and Sobrante Park. Murder Dubbs is where I'm from . . . better known as the Rolling 20s, selling rock cocaine, pimping, hustling, jacking, and balling.

Bobby Lee's words lifted the mood of the service; his voice on the page magically came alive and he was back to being the resilient fellow we remembered him as. Afterwards, we were approached by some inmates who introduced themselves as Bobby's homeboys. They politely requested a copy of Bobby Lee's writings to pass on to Bobby's mother. While regulations prevented us from exchanging contact information with the guys, we did slip them our dog-eared, folded copies of Bobby Lee's emboldened words. We walked back to our car without much to say. It looked as if another anonymous inmate soul had left San Quentin quietly. Or so we thought.

Bobby Lee's death subsequently prompted a flurry of local Bay Area news coverage. The Fox Oakland/San Francisco TV outlet—KTVU—picked up on the story and aired a multipart investigative piece scrutinizing the entire California state prison medical system. Bobby's death caused ripples inside the CDCR (California Department of Corrections and Rehabilitation) system. An on-call doctor who collected a six-figure overtime-laden salary during the incident was put under scrutiny. Next, U.S. District Court Judge Thelton Henderson named an outside trustee to take over the entire prison medical system citing, "incompetence and outright depravity in the rendering of medical care." Bobby's mother—a retired Oakland nurse—filed a wrongful death lawsuit on behalf of Bobby's five-year-old daughter.

Sadly for Bobby Lee, the edifice of a brand new San Quentin medical facility came years too late. As we drive past the facility every Friday at dusk, our thoughts flash to Bobby Lee, that former warrior from Acorns, 69 Village, and Funk Town, sitting by the classroom door and just taking it all in.

That very door that Bobby sat next to became the portal to a whole new world for us as writers and as men.

CHAPTER 2

The New Men in Black

You never forget your first visit to San Quentin because the feeling you have going inside for the very first time is the same feeling that sticks in your craw the 320th time you go in. The place has a presence that, no matter how many times you cross San Quentin's front East Gate into the prison, you feel the looming history of one of the most famous penitentiaries in the world.

San Quentin State Prison was originally built *by* inmates *for* inmates during the mid-nineteenth century. Before opening its gates in the summer of 1852, the inmate workforce who built San Quentin lived in squalor on prison ships anchored off Point San Quentin. Today, the prison utilizes 275 of its allotted 435 acres, prime Marin County waterfront property that real estate developers have slobbered over for the past several decades. Land value alone is estimated at over $600 million, not counting the massive environmental clean-up issues (asbestos) that would be required should the state knuckle under and convert the land into upscale housing.

San Quentin's inmate population waivers below 5,000 inmates, with 740 living inside California's one and only Death Row (for men). After 1995, California switched its means of execution from

gas chamber to lethal injection while housing a condemned population that includes Richard Allen Davis (the murderer of young Polly
Klaas in 1993), Richard Ramirez ("the Night Stalker," AC/DC's
most notorious fan), and Scott Petersen (convicted of decapitat-
ing his pregnant wife, Lacey, on Christmas Eve 2002). Besides its
Death Row clientele, San Quentin has celebrated alumni that include Black Panther Eldridge Cleaver, Robert Kennedy assassin
Sirhan Sirhan, country star Merle Haggard, Charles Manson, por-
nographer Jim Mitchell, jazz saxophonist Art Pepper, composer
Henry Cowell (jailed on "morals" charges during the late thirties),
and black revolutionary George Jackson.

When we first began our work at San Quentin, we knew that
unique programs existed there—like the *San Quentin News,* which is
one of the only regularly published prison newspapers in the world.
Or San Quentin TV, which operates a staff of inmate filmmakers.
San Quentin's Prison University Project is one of the only degree-
granting college courses in the state. The San Quentin Giants have
a longtime association with the San Francisco Giants organization,
who donate uniforms and equipment. Being in close proximity to
Marin, Alameda, and Contra Costa counties provides San Quentin
with an army of both religious and secular volunteers who create
and run the scores of educational and social programs for little or
no pay. While San Quentin isn't the Ritz, many a convict would
prefer doing time there than at another prison not only because of
the desirable Northern California climate, but also because of the
educational and social programs designed to help prisoners prepare
for their release to the outside world.

Once our required background checks were cleared by the state,
and after presenting ID and signing in at the main gate, we ventured down the walkway path to meet with the prison's education
coordinator, Jean Bracy. The stunning view from inside the rather
mundane employee snack bar was something restaurateur Wolf-
gang Puck would envy: a picturesque vista punctuated by the Rich-

mond San Rafael Bridge amid a waterway replete with freighters, boats, and the Larkspur ferry line vessels crammed with alcohol-imbibing commuters.

We met Jean Bracy clutching a couple of copies of our books, including *Hell's Angel*. We quickly told our story: how, as writers, we'd worked with criminals, punk rockers, and other historically edgy people. Yet neither were we ourselves bikers or felons, nor had we ever been arrested. After coffee and a quick chat, Ms. Bracy was suitably impressed enough to offer us a tour of North Block, San Quentin's top-of-the-hill lifer cell block. We figured that if Ms. Bracy turned down our offer to start up a writing class, at least we'd scored a cook's tour of the place where our father had visited, and where Johnny Cash had performed Bob Dylan's "Wanted Man," as well as "San Quentin" and, of course, "A Boy Named Sue."

Most of our San Quentin touchstones were purely from the arts. As we walked past the doorways and sally ports, we thought of Art Pepper, one of the greatest jazz saxophonists. Art was a hopeless dope fiend and part of the elite West Coast school of hepcat bebop players that included Chet Baker and Gerry Mulligan. Art did two hitches at Q (San Quentin) for heroin possession and addiction during the sixties, which he elaborates on in his extraordinary autobiography, *Straight Life*.

In addition to Cash and Pepper, we flashed on one of our favorite writers, Edward Bunker (Eddie), known to avid fans of the Quentin Tarantino film *Reservoir Dogs* as Mr. Blue. Eddie's book, *Education of a Felon,* is a must-read primer on prison life that gives a sparklingly clear view of life inside San Quentin during the late forties and fifties. At 17, Bunker was once the youngest inmate in San Quentin's history. His visceral books and other writings were later successfully adapted to film, resulting in *Straight Time*, starring Dustin Hoffman, a stern, unflinching cinematic look inside the mind of a criminal on parole, and *Animal Factory,* adapted and directed by Steve Buscemi, apparently set in San Quentin but filmed in Philadelphia.

Animal Factory is one of the more bizarre (albeit accurate) prison films because of its over-the-top depictions of prison subcultures, including Mickey Rourke's portrayal of Jan the Actress, an incarcerated transsexual.

We immediately found San Quentin to be one of those classic love/hate environments. For everyone, from the wardens to the inmates, San Quentin is chock full of contradiction. "San Quentin, I hate every inch of you," Cash sneered. And after you visit or spend any amount of time there, you really do hate every inch of the place. Yet at the same time, you kind of respect it, and, truth be told, learn to love it a little.

First stop on our tour: the famed North Block dining hall. As we entered, the steel door closed and locked behind us. Then the humidity slapped us in the face. Stretched across the dining hall were group tables, each with four protruding bolted seats around an octagonal stainless steel tabletop. Over in the far corner, we spied a couple of muscular inmates exercising. Not on treadmills and stair-climbers, but by duckwalking across the room Chuck Berry–style, with knees bent and arms extended, holding enormous plastic buckets filled with water. It was an ingenious but strenuous regimen they'd devised in response to the much publicized ban on weight piles over a decade before. When behind bars in California, exercise consists of isometrics, push-ups, and burpees—hands on the floor in front of you, kick back your legs into a push-up position, then immediately return to your feet. Burpees alone can keep a guy in a modicum of good shape.

Up in North Block, the dining hall wasn't, at first glance, much to look at—one big room, lots of noise, sweltering heat, the smell of perspiration and chow—until we noticed the walls. There were six fifty-year-old murals painted by an inmate named Alfredo Santos, *each* twelve by one hundred feet, painted on "canvases" of granite walls. Santos's murals are an Expressionistic panoramic history of California crammed into one huge room, not in living color, but bathed in brown sepia, once carelessly restored with slapped-on layers of clear-coat.

The murals chronologically depict California's history of Spanish conquistadors, Native and Mexican Americans, Franciscan missionaries, covered wagons lumbering west, an assembly line constructing a World War II fighter plane, a rodeo, and a Hollywood premiere with Chaplin and Groucho. Some swear that the eyes of the mural subjects follow you around the room. The artist's style is surreal: Diego Rivera meets Salvador Dali meets *MAD* magazine's Sergio Aragonés. Could this be the place where Johnny and June sang "Jackson" and "Darlin' Companion," and where Johnny rolled out "A Boy Named Sue" and "San Quentin" for the first time? Turns out that was another chow hall on the premises. Still, the murals are dramatic enough on their own.

The second, and less aesthetically interesting, wonder of our North Block tour were the actual jail tiers, an old-fashioned multi-leveled cell block, not much different from the set that Elvis and his hepcat cons danced on during the choreographed scene in *Jailhouse Rock*. While the aura of Johnny and June, Art, and Eddie touched us inside our first visit to San Quentin, walking outside to the North Block tier was like time-traveling back to the days of Bogey, Cagney, and George Raft. The high-decibel chatter of confinement, along with the ever-present smell of stale perspiration, made it hard to imagine living there 24/7.

On the bottom tier, one of the cell doors was ajar.

"Wanna go inside?" our friendly CO (correctional officer) escort asked us, motioning towards the open unoccupied cell.

"Sure, why not?" we muttered to each other, shrugging. Except we were thinking, who lives here? Whose home is this? Are we intruding? What if they come back?

With nary a whit of concern, the CO shoved the inmate's clothes aside. He pulled down a T-shirt that hung between the cell door and the stainless steel sink and toilet, erected for privacy purposes.

"That's not supposed to be up there," the CO said, snatching the shirt and tossing it on the floor. A television encased in transparent plastic signified this inmate as one of the lucky ones. He had a limited broadcast link to the outside world. Unfortunately he also had a cellie close enough to be breathing the same thick air.

We sat on the cell bunk for only a moment, claustrophobic and spooked. The combination of the heat and the ambience took an immediate toll on your nerves. Our CO guide slammed the door. We looked at each other, nervously thinking,

What the hell are we getting ourselves into?

If anything, our tour of North Block taught us one basic rule: our writing class *had* to be hip—*and cutting edge*—different from the other programs like Alcoholics and Narcotics Anonymous or Anger Management. Unlike university creative writing students, prison inmates have seen and lived a lot. Prison is a place where inmates have their bullshit detectors permanently set to level ten. Classroom agendas needed to be completely responsive to the present moment. Whether our students had robbed or beaten people up, whether they had grown or sold dope, whether they'd stolen cars, hacked computers, or embezzled stocks and bonds, we didn't care. We had to blow their minds with each class. We needed to create a weekly event that would help get them *and* us through another crazy week. Once Ms. Bracy gave us the thumbs-up to begin, we would be all-in with a vengeance.

We got the thumbs-up from Bracy in January 2003. We needed to apply to take "Brown Card Instruction," which consisted of a four-hour orientation class taught by San Quentin insiders educating volunteers on how to deal with inmates and the prison environment. Bracy then informed us that our writing class would not be taught to lifers up on North Block. Instead, we would be relegated to a different area of the prison called H-Unit.

"What's an H-Unit?" we asked politely.

H-Unit was a lower security lockdown zone located in the back end of the prison. While the main prison blocks and wards were a shorter, breezier stroll from the main gate entrance (complete with the panoramic San Francisco Bay view to your left), H-Unit was nearly a mile hoof—seven-tenths, to be exact—down a small bumpy road that snaked around the side and into the back of the prison complex where there was no Marin County bayside vista visible from inside the yard. H-Unit was also an underserved area of San Quentin in terms of educational programs. Most of the volunteer academic action was happening up on the hill for the Lifers, while H-Unit was a forgotten bastard sector.

H-Unit was designed to house the Short-Timers, as opposed to the Lifers and the condemned convicts situated up on the hill. Short-Timers were the guys sentenced to five years or less, or inmates who had returned to SQ custody to serve out a few bonus months or weeks as parole violators, mostly for drug-related offenses.

H-Unit started out as a Tent City back in 1985 when new prison construction was banned by the legislature in California. So overcrowded inmates lived in U.S. Army surplus tents. H-Unit is now five single-story concrete barracks (with bunks, not cells) dotted along the perimeter of a dusty, barren, rectangular dirt prison yard. Although it was nicknamed the "Going Home" section of the prison, H-Unit was not a particularly popular place for most cons to do time. Most would rather serve their sentences languishing in a two-to-a-cell than share an upper and lower bunk with another bunkie in a more open setting. The barracks, or "dorms" as they were called, represented a downgrade in privacy and overall comfort. Generally cells were preferred.

We accepted Mrs. Bracy's offer to teach in H-Unit and selected Friday nights from 6:30 to 8:30 P.M. to debut our new class, "Creative Writing: Finding Your Voice on the Page."

If we were gonna be the New Men in Black, we had to accessorize appropriately: black jeans, dark shirts, black jackets, shades when it was sunny, and above all, hip shoes. Like a businessman's power tie, shoes are the inmate's sole form of self-expression. We had learned two things from previous writing clients about the joint: that shoes made the man and that, generally, inmates were scammers out to score what they could from you.

Meanwhile, serious questions remained. Were we ready, and at what level should we teach: middle school, high school, college? And at what tempo should we teach—fast or slow? Could the guys keep up with us? Could we keep up with *them*? It was time to find out.

One last thing about JC. Johnny Cash totally "got" San Quentin, within three basic levels of consciousness—head, heart, and gut.

Contrary to what most folks believe, Johnny didn't do a day of prison time. The scar in the corner of his mouth came from a careless doctor, not a street brawl. According to his own lore, he did a fictitious night in the Starkville City Jail for picking flowers, except the real truth was that he spent one night in an El Paso jail cell for possession of thousands of pep pills smuggled in from Juarez before beating the rap.

Johnny Cash used his "head" by harnessing the power generated by convicts locked down in old-school joints like Folsom and San Quentin and incorporating their energy back into his music. At Folsom and San Quentin, he entertained and inspired the inmates without exploitation while simultaneously reinventing himself. Would San Quentin serve as the same catalyst of reinvention for us? We hoped so.

Cash had "heart," and communicated heart-to-heart through his music. We soon learned that prison inmates can spot a phony in a millisecond, and that a criminal's stock in trade—for better or for worse—is his (or her) talent to read people in an instant. Merle Haggard tells the story of how Cash, from the San Quentin stage, imitated a cranky CO standing nearby who was chomping on a big wad of chewing gum. From that moment, Johnny captured the hearts of the entire audience. We needed to pass the same test of authenticity.

Johnny Cash communicated passion and humanity through his music, a "gut" punch beat of "boom-chucka-boom-chucka-boom-chucka," using twangy rockabilly guitar chords, a kicking bass line, and a simple drum backbeat. We needed to tap into that same gut level of simplicity while our students searched to find their voices on the page to convincingly recreate the "gravel in the guts and the spit in the eye" that Cash often sang about.

Up until his death in 2003, when his music reverted back to its most primal acoustic elements under the tutelage of producer Rick Rubin, Cash continued to utilize his head, heart, and gut. We figured that if we were lucky enough to fire on those same three cylinders, we too might command the respect needed to make our prison class a success.

CHAPTER 3

Groucho Marxists

In some ways, getting inside a prison is as difficult as getting out of one.

We exaggerate, of course, but once we were green-lighted to start up our class in the first quarter of 2003 we needed to go through the necessary steps to gain regular weekly access. First, we needed to know the rules. To learn the rules, we had to be trained. And to get trained, we were required to attend an annual four-hour course at San Quentin that granted us state volunteer employee status, which made us subject to obeying the rules, and which also made us subject to severe punishment if we were stupid enough to knowingly break any of their rules.

Once a month, nearly a hundred stout-hearted people cram into a San Quentin training facility to attend mandatory access training. Latecomers who expect a vacant seat are SOL. The course was designed to alert volunteers on the do's and don't's of operating a class or meeting inside the walls. After we were properly trained—voila!—the prison presented us with a picture ID which provided us access to San Quentin's various yards and classrooms. We were now "armed" and dangerous.

With "the card," if you have legitimate business (as opposed to just hangin' with the homies), you have surprisingly broad access, short of places like Death Row, the dreaded gothic Adjustment Center (home of the most dangerous and violent incorrigibles who can't function properly on Death Row), and Ad(ministrative) Seg(regation) a.k.a. the Hole. Unlike your American Express, your coveted ID card lives at the front gate, checked out to you as you arrive, and then checked back in as you leave.

We soon learned that you don't *ever* want to lose your ID card. Losing "the card" inside is far, far worse than losing a credit card or a cell phone in the civilian world. Immediately we heard the stories. One teacher had lost his. Losing an ID card will result in a massive inmate search and lockdown. Picture hundreds of inmates pulled from their bunks or cells and aggressively searched while having to stand around in the rain, the cold, or the hot sun. Not a great way to endear yourself to several hundred potential hardcore criminal students.

Turned out, the required training class was extremely democratic. *Everybody*, old hands and newbies, must renew once a year to maintain their access status. The class itself is like traffic school: you think you don't need it, but afterwards, you leave a better driver. Same thing with prison access training: it's a good idea to renew your perspective with lessons taught by a collection of teachers, administrators, assistant wardens, and CO's who have walked the line for years. We soon deduced that the moment you're too comfortable walking a prison yard is the moment you should consider staying away for good.

In correctional code, paid and volunteer teachers were known as "free staff"; inmates taking those classes while doing time were "programming." The demographics of the volunteers were wide, from old-timers to church folks to university students who offer college tutoring. We joined the Jesuit monks in brown robes, the Happy Catholics or "the Jesus Christ-ers" (the latter being Gore Vidal's term, not ours) toting folk guitars, the grizzled 12-steppers, ex-felons, former drunks and dope addicts, anger management specialists, reentry and family counselors, community activists, doctors, nutritionists, baseball coaches, and tennis players. All are expected to learn the rules and regs and abide by them. At first it was a little like Groucho Marxism—not wanting to be a part of any organization that would stoop to having us as members. But soon we took our place amongst the army of Marin County do-gooders, and resigned ourselves to the fact that we, too, had become do-gooders.

As volunteers-in-training, we noticed that men and women were represented equally. While it was heartening in a way, we weren't so sure we'd encourage *our* female loved ones to go inside. Call us old-fashioned, but we suggest women might consider seeking out a female facility. Female inmates are actually in need of more support than their male counterparts. We learned that with male inmates, their women and family members usually stand by them with phone calls, letters of support, conjugal visits, and money deposited into canteen accounts, whereas incarcerated female inmates are forgotten and ostracized by their families and partners. In one California institution, Valley Center, near Chowchilla, only a small percentage of female inmates receive one single visitor per year.

As we learned during training, a whole bevy of rules govern "appropriate dress." Verboten clothing is the surest way of getting turned away at the front gate of any prison. Besides inappropriately sexy clothing, particularly on women, most of the rules regarding clothing revolve around color. Colors, in our society, have grown into powerful symbols of gangs and subcultures. Later we would learn not to carry the red or blue railroad handkerchiefs that signify gang ties and colors. Shirts and hats with logos may also fall under violation. San Francisco Giants hats, okay. Chicago White Sox or Oakland Raiders caps, not so okay. Other examples: wearing anything blue especially denim, wearing green or camouflage resembling the colors worn by the correctional officers, or wearing orange, the hue worn by newly-arrived convicts in "reception" who are awaiting dispersal to another institution, are all not allowed. During the rainy season, inmates wear the yellow vinyl raincoats many of us wore in school, so anything yellow is also out.

In other words, wear black, all black, like the Men in Black.

The main idea is to blend in and *not* attract the attention of the officer sitting in the gun tower, who will instantly notice someone wearing the same colors as an inmate and may assume you're a prisoner "out of bounds" and walking where you ought not be walking.

Other fashion no-no's include loose athletic sweats or open-toed shoes or sandals. As previously mentioned, for reasons of self-expression, shoes are king in prison—they're the first article of clothing an inmate notices. A good rule of thumb on shoes: if you can't run in them, you shouldn't wear them. However, by the way, running in a prison yard is against the rules, since it connotes being chased, and being chased risks someone getting shot or gassed. *Never* run in a prison yard.

Going into a prison is like stepping into a time machine and time-traveling backward twenty years. It's an environment where there are few computers, virtually no laptops (you definitely don't want prison inmates with Internet access), and a place where cell phones are a supreme no-no. Cell phones go for a premium on the prison black market and are the most common search targets. As lifelong carriers of pocketknives since our days as Cub Scouts, we had to break our habit of toting a blade, particularly a lock-blade knife.

We learned quickly that if you feel the need to snap a picture inside prison with a camera or a phone, don't. Cameras—still or video—unless you're a cleared member of the press, are strictly forbidden. Other items on the prison shit list included: gum (used to jam locks), dental floss, fishing line or binding wire (used to strangle victims), non-collapsible umbrellas (used as lances), or wallets and purses bulging with personal information, private addresses, credit cards, and cash.

Oddly, prison is the one place on earth where cash money is essentially useless, unless it's circulated on the black market for dope or tobacco. Otherwise, prison is a place where Top Ramen soup and postage stamps are primary currency.

Financially, it doesn't take much to survive in prison, while emotionally, it does. Two hundred dollars a month dumped in a "canteen account" towards food and toiletries goes a long, long way, even in facilities where inmates are routinely charged for basics like toilet paper and soap. For many prisoners, a trip to the canteen represents the only free-willed decision they'll make all week. For sale at the canteen is stuff that civilians like us take for granted: items like dry soup packets (ramen), processed snack foods (chips and crackers), cookies, pints of ice cream (Haagen Dazs), scented shampoo, and other optional staples that are made available for purchase. The assembled goods are often referred to as "packages." We soon learned that two things you don't mess with on a prisoner's schedule are their medication and the time they need to retrieve their packages. In Texas alone, in 2010, the prison system sold a whopping 33 million 25-cent packages of ramen noodles to the tune of $8.3 million. That's a lot of soup *and* currency, though you won't hear Top Ramen cop to it.

By far the biggest pitfall and liability that prison officials worry about in terms of volunteerism is over-familiarity between the inmates and volunteers. Not counting the potential man/woman sexual attraction thing (which we soon found out does happen), well-meaning volunteers can be targeted by hustlers, users, and sweet-talkers. Smuggling, whether its drugs, food items, or electronics, can be a dangerous but lucrative income supplement, but it can also land volunteers in the classroom . . . as fellow inmates! Unlike with the bikers we had written about who like to embrace and kiss, most body contact is forbidden in prison. Handshakes are cool, especially our favorite, the gripped "forearm shake" favored by Native American inmates. The Obama fist bump soon became our preferential form of greeting: quick, hip, and sanitary.

Compared to the other state institutions, San Quentin enjoys an embarrassment of educational riches, especially in comparison to the other institutions inside the California penal system. Fortunately for Californians, most of the educational programs that have survived inside Q are privately funded and don't cost the taxpayers a dime. Inside San Quentin, scores of courses—gardening, yoga, baseball and tennis, accredited GED, college, and self-help courses—and even cultural events like theater exist for inmates bright enough to want to better themselves. The unwritten rule on the H-Unit yard is that the classroom is a sanctuary—much like the religious chapel—where inmates trying to better themselves through education are not to be targeted for violence or retribution, at least not while sitting inside of it.

One of the things inmates seem to need most, besides a high school diploma or access to college courses, is basic "life" education. During our initial training, it became clear that prison is full of men who are behind the eight ball in the simplest aspects of life management skills—responsibilities that most of us take for granted, like paying the electric bill, balancing a checkbook, maintaining decent credit, shopping for food, or worse, avoiding overindulgence. Want to see firsthand the effects of the pharmaceutical and distillery industries on a portion of our population that's deficient in basic sound judgment? Come to prison.

CHAPTER 4

This Thing of Ours

When we received word from Ms. Bracy that we had been granted permission to teach at San Quentin, it came with a major caveat: she suggested that we not take on any inmates as clients or write anyone's memoirs, which was okay with us. Our idea was to get them to do their own writing. We were invited to enlist as volunteers for a fledgling start-up project ironically called the Success Program. Bracy explained that the Success Program was then-warden Jeanne Woodford's pet educational project. Woodford, with 30 years experience as a correctional officer and administrator, was a progressive warden who'd been appointed in 1999. The Success Program was formed to serve San Quentin's H-Unit.

By 2002 Woodford's Success Program had accumulated a few volunteer courses—mostly of the self-help variety, including Anger Management & Substance Abuse meetings, Landscaping & Gardening, and Parenting instruction. If an inmate demonstrated himself free of any prison or outside gang affiliations and hadn't been written up for any recent episodes of bad behavior, he would be qualified to enroll in the Success Program. Although these were not yet college- or high school-accredited courses, Success students who completed a quarter of a class would receive a parchment certificate and a signed, gold-colored completion form called a "chronos" from their instructor, which they could insert into their personal files to demonstrate that they were programming and making an effort towards rehabilitation. By offering our class through Woodford's Success Program we could enjoy the services of the inmate clerks who would process the necessary weekly attendance sheets and oversee the quarterly registration process.

Our "Finding Your Voice on the Page" class wasn't exactly compatible with the lineup of self-improvement classes offered by Success. Truth was, we weren't interested in curbing drug and alcohol use or discouraging aberrant antisocial behavior. We only wanted to demystify the whole notion of being a writer, revealing it as something anybody can pick up or achieve, utilizing prison inmates as guinea pigs to test our new teaching ideas. Besides, who would listen to us about personal morality anyway? At home, our bookshelves and record collections were crammed with the works of social deviants, drug addicts, and drunks whose work we cherished and admired. Guys like Miles Davis, Art Pepper, Eddie Bunker, Social Distortion, and Johnny Cash.

Our class was designed to serve two immediate, self-serving purposes: To help us acquire some quick teaching experience so we could seek out more secure gigs at a college or university, and, if these students didn't end up being dolts or idiots, then maybe the class would inspire *us* creatively. We were just two writer dudes pushing words out the door for a living, and after two years pounding out 80,000-word manuscripts, we were feeling a little secluded working on our own. Yet neither of us was prepared to swallow our pride and return to the traditional office workplace where we could look forward to gossiping around the water cooler and sitting through tedious budget and staff meetings.

Jean Bracy dutifully assigned Steve Emerick, who managed the arts curriculum up on the hill, to help us acclimate to the penitentiary environment. Steve lived on the San Quentin premises in a modest house, which the state of California provided to lucky members of the SQ staff, with his wife and toddler. Steve had joined San Quentin a year prior, and had carved out quite an admirable niche for himself. He had taken a large, old, cluttered storage room, and with the help of the brawn of inmates anxious to avoid the grinding boredom of incarceration, gutted its entire contents and turned the antique space into an impressive ad hoc arts office and loft. Steve knew how to jiggle the system and had scored himself a small budget to hire part-time instructors to teach arts and crafts, painting, drawing, and other artful endeavors. He had already hired an experienced creative writing teacher for the men up on the hill. As volunteers we would not be paid to teach our H-Unit class—which didn't bother us one way or the other. It only made us more anxious to come up with a radical concept that would contrast with the more traditional creative writing classes we'd taken at U.C. Berkeley night school before we'd gotten published.

Starting with a blank canvas, we envisioned our class as an educational end around. Learn by doing; create a charismatic experience. We needed to create a writing environment that was so exclusive, experimental, and appealing that students would get hooked into showing up each and every week—as if it were a drug like heroin. Our target audience knew a thing or two about addiction. As we'd emphasized to Ms. Bracy, we hoped our affiliation with Sonny Barger as co-writers might give us a leg up on the savvy, often-manipulative, sometimes mind-bending, hardened criminals they warned us about at the brown card instructional training.

First order would be to strike a bargain with our students: we'll share our firsthand world of publishing and writing with you if you share your world of doing time with us. We weren't entering San Quentin as faux bikers or wannabe-bad-boy-tough-guys. Although we had worked quite closely with edgy "literary clients" and helped tell their unique and often thrilling tales, we never rode motorcycles with Sonny Barger nor did we try to drink Johnny Rotten under the table at his local pub. As writers, we did what poet Quincy Troupe had once advised us to do: Submerge your ego! "This is not about you, this is about them," he said. We would take that same "curious observer" stance we used writing books to this new class.

Next, we were assigned one of the few remaining time slots. We picked Fridays right after six o'clock chow and after the final head count of the day had cleared. Yet as soon as we committed to Friday night writing, we second-guessed our choice of time slot. Who the hell would give up their T.G.I.F. evenings out on the yard to sign up for a creative writing class? In addition, our wives weren't too thrilled to hear the news that Friday nights at home and on the town were cancelled in favor of their husbands' spending time behind bars and razor wire teaching felons how to write. But they trusted us on this one. Plus we fervently promised them that we would phone home the minute we drove out the gate to make sure we hadn't been held hostage or been stabbed and discarded in some dark, forgotten corridor.

The first week, we had no earthly idea what to expect. While we were warned up front that most state prison inmates were functionally illiterate with various learning disabilities, that wasn't what concerned us. Forget grammar and spelling—that's why God invented spell check. We accepted the challenge to sign up as many men of all ages and races as possible—men coming from homes where education was not encouraged. Chances were, their parents—if they had any around at all—had been too loaded or drunk, out hustling the streets themselves, or trapped toiling in low-paying jobs with zero benefits to worry about their kids' schooling. Prison is the home of America's fallen rejects: the crack cocaine and meth casualties who live among the junkies, winos, pimps, and whores in urban wastelands like East Oakland and Compton, or the backwoods burnouts from the pot farms of Humboldt and Lake Counties where the white-collar, pot-card-carrying elite pot smokers get their smoke.

We agreed: we'd take 'em all. But here was the twist: What if we could actually balance out the uneducated underachievers with the clever, calculating, and intelligent street-smart felons who had the potential to become highly capable wordsmiths? Here was a group with an overabundance of colorful and vivid life experiences to draw from and write about. What if we found a few budding Eddie Bunker street writers or the next articulate Eldridge Cleaver type to buoy the quality of the class? One could only dream.

We soon found that the vast majority of indigent H-Unit prisoners came from the scrap heap of broken families. Even more came from our broken public school system. We weren't about to bullshit these lumpenproletariats by downplaying the advantages of learning and bettering yourself through self-expression and the written word. Instead, we thought about the comment attributed to the famous TV and movie personality Mr. T of the A-Team. Whenever jocks and tough guys invited Mr. T to pump iron with them at the local gym, he would retort, "Why don't you come down with me and work out at the library?"

Before ramping up our planning, we checked up on the creative writing class Steve had set up on the hill for North Block and West Block. Then we sat in on a university extension course in San Francisco. It was taught by a diligent college instructor. Her curriculum was extensive and resembled the creative writing courses we had previously taken on the adult college extension circuit. Those were generally comprised of about 12 students. During the first hour, pupils would receive customary instruction on proper literary technique, and then perform a short writing exercise to sharpen their styles. The second half of the class involved reading other students' works-in-progress, and discussing and critiquing their ongoing work. One of the main things rookie writers must figure out: Are my story lines and narratives making any sense, and is the reader getting the emotional drift of what I'm feeling or trying to convey?

We decided to veer "this thing of ours" (or as the Italians call it, *la cosa nostra*) in a different direction. First off, forget a dozen students. We wanted to double that. (We've always been "butts in seats" kind of guys.) And since there were two of us, and prison was such an overpowering, intimidating environment anyway, why not capitalize on a team-teaching method? Previously when we'd staged and conducted conventions and symposiums during our previous lives in the radio/music world, we regularly featured two co-hosts— Keith or Kent and/or someone from radio or the record business to work as a twosome. It worked. (Radio folks with on-air experience were fantastic co-hosts in front of crowds.) Audience participation was key.

During our years hosting music conventions, we had employed "unconventional" ways of staging events. Rather than headline a speaker to talk for an hour, we would arrange a one-on-one multimedia interview. We would debut new music through a "Jukebox Jury" format (similar to the British TV show in the 1960s) where a group of radio programmers would evaluate and rate new, unheard songs, grading them on a point scale, after which we would determine the top three winners in total points. As we learned in the music biz during our tenure with *Gavin,* it was more fun using a walk-around-the-room Oprah-Montel tag-team approach with an audience, as opposed to moderators stuck onstage sitting behind a table with a name tent card, pontificating behind a microphone.

The same might apply to this new classroom experience. Our teaching philosophy became: want an interesting and more exciting class? Kick the teacher's ass out from behind the desk and have them walk the line and interact with the students in the room.

Modern teaching and learning trends today justify a social and interactive experience—especially in today's nonstop 24/7 multimedia short-attention-span blitz. Ever watch brainiac college students complaining on YouTube about the archaic university teaching structure that's stuck in nineteenth-century methodology? They have a point! With rote knowledge generously available online and specifically through search engines, Web sites, Wikipedia, and blogs, scholarly learning habits need to be revamped and adjusted. Why should a young person pay exorbitant tuition to be droned to by some tenured college professor, or worse, by his or her teaching assistant? If we wanted to show this contrarian generation of students a thing or two, we'd give them an addictive and interactive classroom experience that involves each and every person in the room.

"Today's child is bewildered when he enters the nineteenth-century environment that still characterizes the educational establishment where information is scarce but ordered and structured by fragmented, classified patterns, subjects and schedules." That's a quote from media and communications theorist Marshal McLuhan from 1967, and it's still relevant today!

That said, what if we came up with a new concept of teaching writing and tested it on prison inmates? Why not pull out the stops? These were criminals and convicts for heaven's sake. And what a motley crew to work with: criminals—with more chaotic life experience, antisocial behavior, and hard luck personal tales at their fingertips than a roomful of law-abiding wannabe novelists and rookie college writing students. We wanted this thing of ours—'Finding Your Voice on the Page"—to be the edgiest academic experience anyone could muster.

Funny thing. While researching the various $20,000 Master of Fine Arts (MFA) two-year writing degrees, we noticed that the majority of the tenured professors in post-secondary—i.e., college level—creative writing didn't offer that much frontline information about the *publishing* business—how to deal with pressured editors, crusty agents, and screwed up manuscripts. It's one thing to read Raymond Carver's exquisite short stories as examples of unattainable expertise, but how about explaining what makes a good literary proposal that will sell and help you pay the rent?

In our experience, the old, albeit flawed, adage, "Those who can, do. Those who can't, teach," had some traction. Quite often we'd found that published instructors fell into three categories: 1) the occasional or neophyte novelist; 2) academes like Ross from TV's *Friends* whose doctoral thesis was published by a university press and stashed on a dusty library shelf; or 3) writers who contribute articles and fiction to obscure literary reviews or tiny indie publishing houses.

In other words, with their degrees, doctorates, fellowships, awards, grants, and scholarships, many professors were more teacher than writer, more hat than cattle. Few teachers we knew lived off the blank page like we had to. Few worked directly with large New York houses desperate to make their quarterly numbers, who specialized in pop culture written in the genre that Manhattan editors fancifully refer to as "narrative nonfiction."

There was a twist of irony in this: while we wanted to implement more modern and experimental techniques to stimulate learning, we were being thrown into an environment that was completely devoid of any modern amenities found in even the most primitive junior college classrooms. Indispensable techno devices like Internet connections, cell phones, laptop computers, iPods, iPads, iPhones, Droids, BlackBerries, or any variety of other electronic devices were ALL banned in prison. And for good reason: the distressing thought of these guys in lockdown possessing black market Internet devices and stealth cell phone access is an unnerving, and thankfully unlawful, scenario.

At the time we were given the green light to debut the class, we had just released two new book projects, one being Sonny Barger's first action pulp novel, called *Dead in 5 Heartbeats*, published by William Morrow, featuring a rogue motorcycle antihero protagonist named Patch Kinkade. The second project was a book called *Soul on Bikes*, the true story of an all-black, all-Harley motorcycle club from Oakland called the East Bay Dragons. The book was told from the point of view of its founder and leader, Tobie Levingston, an honorable and stalwart leader. To this day, *SOB* is one of our favorite books that we've written.

While we enjoyed working on both book projects, we were concerned that our writing might be strictly typecast as biker and motorcycle lit. Yet, walking among the biker types, many of whom had done time themselves, did help prepare us for what we were about to experience at San Quentin.

On April 11, 2003 at 5:00 P.M., we walked up to San Quentin's East Gate to teach our very first creative writing class. Although it was a bright Indian summer day, SQ's East Gate resembled the entrance to a busy nightclub more than it did a foreboding prison. Standing outside waiting to be let in were a smiling, blissful-looking troupe of "Happy Catholics," a half-dozen clean-cut men and women, plus a few college-aged people who congregated and gleefully chatted amongst themselves as they signed their names on a roving clipboard, clutching their acoustic guitar cases. These folks had arrived to conduct the six o'clock Friday night folk mass held up on the hill. Standing next to them were a couple of somber bearded forty-something's dressed in black (just like us). They stoically clutched their AA handbooks as they awaited entrance. Nearby was a trio of older executive types wearing Dockers and pressed Brooks Brothers shirts, most likely the same age as our father, Joe, when he'd first visited SQ. Except for the AA or NA guys, everybody seemed to be very comfortable and in lively spirits as they talked amongst themselves.

We, in contrast, were seriously nervous wrecks.

The black correctional officer running the gate wore dark Ray-Bans and was built like an NFL linebacker. He was the bouncer holding the all-important VIP list at an exclusive discothèque nightclub, and he had his routine down pat. He processed each visitor, who either gained entrance via a prearranged gate pass shown on the computer or had a brown card ID waiting there on file. In between signing in volunteers, he waved in each car or delivery vehicle coming in and out of the prison. For every car that exited the prison, he would inspect their open trunk and then send them on their way. People came and went, including visitors and CO's coming on and off duty.

The CO at the gate gave us the sign-in clipboard. In exchange we surrendered our driver's licenses, and once we finished signing in he handed us back our California licenses along with two brand-new, shining laminated brown card ID's sporting our dour faces.

He looked down at our names and faces and then glared back over at us. "You guys brothers or something?"

"Twins," we grunted nervously, as he handed Keith Kent's ID, and Kent Keith's ID. He'd given up on sorting out who was who. We couldn't blame him.

As we turned to shuffle off into the direction of H-Unit, Kent courteously asked the CO, "Sir, is this where we catch the shuttle down to H-Unit, sir?"

The CO shook his head. "Good luck trying to grab one of those babies after five o'clock."

Rather than wait for the alleged shuttle (whose existence we doubt to this day), we decided to walk down the road to H-Unit.

We eyed the horizon ahead. There was Mt. Tamalpais, towering in the distance as we began walking. As we headed around the first bend, past some prison buildings, down the road toward H-Unit, we spied an unused picnic table behind a cyclone fence surrounded by thorny bushes. Above the table was a large sign printed in red: OFF LIMITS.

Keith pointed at the sign, declaring, "One of these days we gotta have our pictures taken at that table."

"Good luck," Kent replied, "since we can't bring cameras inside."

The sun beat down on us, which gave us an extra layer of sweat beneath our dark clothing. As we strolled down the potholed road towards our final destination, a guard in an old pickup truck pulled up next to us. He yelled out of the open window.

"You guys need a ride?"

We climbed into the truck, speechless, and jumped out at the stop sign not far from the H-Unit entrance. We waved goodbye to the truck as it rolled on towards the convict-run volunteer firehouse. Then we headed to the neat row of houses where Steve Emerick lived, and knocked on his front door. Steve came to the entrance with a shy toddler hanging on to his pant leg.

"You guys are early. Come on in." We took a seat on the couch. The room was littered with preschool educational toys. Steve and the youngster were having a quality father-kid moment that we had just interrupted. We noticed there was no television in the front room. Steve caught on to our observation.

"We don't own a TV."

"Ooookay," said Kent dryly. "Cuts down on the cable bills."

Twenty minutes later, we and Steve walked towards H-Unit and passed a gun tower on the corner. For the last time, we wondered, what in the hell are we doing here anyway? How crazy is this?

The perimeter of H-Unit was lined with two sturdy cyclone fences running parallel, five feet apart with huge bales of razor wire generously woven across the top, upon which a flattened basketball was lodged and impaled. On the ground between the fences were large sharp rocks set in concrete.

"They call them 'leg breakers,'" Steve told us, "In case somebody climbs the first fence, jumps, and attempts an escape."

We walked up to the large double cyclone gate located beneath yet another gun tower. Next to the entrance was a metal box with a white button. Steve pushed the intercom button, which buzzed the officer up inside the adjacent tower. The first of two double-cyclone-fenced double doors creaked slowly open.

We waved at the gun tower. It was an anonymous gesture of thank you to the sharpshooter who had just let us inside the prison complex. We probably seemed like a couple of dumbasses waving "thank you" to an armed guard, somebody we couldn't see. As soon as the first door wheeled shut behind us with a heavy thud, the second cyclone door slowly opened and closed as we stepped inside H-Unit.

CHAPTER 5

First Day of Class

After the second sliding gate closed behind us, we were buzzed into the H-Unit entry area. We signed our names and entry times into a thick guest book. The CO on duty pointed to the airport-style metal detector, which was set on "11." We cleared our pockets, belts, shoes, and hats and the three of us passed through. Next we walked through an open-air no-man's-land passageway called a sally port. At the end was one final buzzered gate that dumped us onto our final destination. We looked out across a vacant prison yard that was half the size of a football field. It was mostly dirt, with a few desperate patches of grass in the middle. Wild ducks and street-smart pigeons swooped in and out of the secured premises, almost as if to say to the inmates, "We're free to come and go, assholes, what's your problem?"

H-Unit featured an unglamorous row of five square dormitory-type barracks. From north to south each "dorm" was numbered with two-foot numerals, 1 through 5. To our far south was another large free-standing structure—the chow hall. Next to the chow hall was a cordoned off area with a small tribal-looking dome structure and a wood-burning campfire pit.

"That's our sweat lodge," said Steve, "for the Native American inmates." Next to the sweat lodge was a lonely, pristine park bench surrounded by colorful, trimmed shrubbery and flowers, a project completed by the Success Program's Gardening and Landscaping class—a tiny patch of paradise situated amid acres of parched earth.

The main yard was uninhabited when we arrived. A spooky silence pervaded. We needed to wait a few minutes until the final count cleared. The last inhabitants of Dorm Five had just sauntered over from the Chow Hall to shuffle back to their bunks in a line and wait for the yard to be opened after six-thirty. A makeshift volleyball court with no net was deserted. Next to it were a couple of pull-up bars. There were no free weights or jogging track. Anybody seen running across or around the yard risked being put down by the sharpshooters posted at each corner position.

We made our way to the main watch station where a small group of CO's wearing camouflage and khaki uniforms patrolled the H-Unit complex. The watch station was adjoined to a square cinder block room which served as the sole education classroom. We picked up our Success roll sheet paperwork from a rack on the wall inside the watch station office. Next to it were two empty holding cells the size of phone booths—known internally as "dummy cages"—with an adjoining sign that stated, "Do not speak to inmates in the holding cells."

We stood out in front of the locked classroom door until a CO pulled out his large ring of thick nickel-plated keys. After rummaging through ten or more keys, he unlocked the metal door of the classroom.

"Which class is this?" asked the CO, half interested.

"Creative Writing," we said in unison, our hearts in our throats. "It's our first day."

The CO shook his head. "Well, make sure you have plenty of Mexicans, otherwise it won't last. These guys don't stick with anything. You might not make it past six weeks." He sensed the impending disappointment in our faces, shrugged and walked away.

We stepped inside what looked to be a run-of-the-mill classroom filled with tables and chairs. Steve grabbed a seat in the back corner of the room.

"I'll sit in for the first half," he said. "Then we give the guys a ten-minute smoke break before the second half."

"Okay." This was it: crunch time. We looked down at our attendance sheet listing about ten names with corresponding CDC numbers. Our hearts sank. Shit. We expected at least 15 to 20.

"I wouldn't worry too much about that," Steve said, trying to comfort us. "You'll get some walk-ups that haven't signed up yet."

"Let's hope," we said, and sighed.

"Next, you need to go next door and have the sergeant announce your class on the yard," Steve instructed.

We checked into the H-Unit Watch Station with our request. He rose up from his desk and grabbed the wireless talking device clipped to his shoulder. He hit the talk button to activate the intercom. His distorted, over-modulated voice boomed across the empty H-Unit yard. Friday chow had just finished and "620," the all-clear code meaning that the count and feeding has been completed, had just been called. Our class was announced over the yard like on the M.A.S.H. television show:

"CREATIVE WRITING! CREATIVE WRITING IN THE EDUCATION CLASSROOM! CREATIVE WRITING IS GOOD!"

In a chain reaction, each CO overseeing each individual dorm one through five repeated the message to the inmates in their bunks as the announcements reverberated and ricocheted around the yard:

CREATIVE WRITING! EDUCATION!
CREATIVE WRITING IN EDUCATION!
CREATIVE WRITING. IN THE CLASSROOM!
620's CLEARED FOR CREATIVE WRITING.
CREATIVE WRITING IS A GO.

Sarge sat back behind his desk and tapped on a slim ledger book sitting next to his phone. "Don't forget to sign in and out. Need to know your whereabouts."

We had already tweaked our lesson plans to suit our tough nut audience. Hello Eddie Bunker; goodbye Gustav Flaubert and Raymond Carver. We brought along our dog-eared copy of Bunker's *Education of a Felon,* which our first editor, Jim Fitzgerald, had worked tirelessly on and his cheeky rewrites intertwined nicely with Bunker's prose, and the classic *Straight Life,* the jazzy memoir of dope and crime by saxophonist Art Pepper who, as previously mentioned, did a couple of stretches at Q himself. (*Straight Life* is the real deal, one of our "bibles," in addition to Quincy Troupe's *Miles* autobio, which we gave Johnny Rotten to read before collaborating with him on his Pistols memoir.)

Our initial strategy for the class was to keep things spontaneous. Share some war stories from the publishing front, or spin a few crazy yarns about the eccentric editors we'd dealt with. Something to give the men a vocational slant on the publishing biz. We thought, why not bring in a DVD dub clip of Edward Norton's self-loathing rant from Spike Lee's *25th Hour* ("F**k you, Montgomery Brogan!") or a timeless George Carlin bit on word usage? (Although there was a TV monitor with a disc player stashed in the corner of the classroom, we found out later, the hard way, not to bring in "uncleared" DVD's or CD's inside the prison.)

Instead of the usual 12 to 15 students in a traditional creative writing university course in the outside world, we figured we could handle 18 to 24 men on the inside. The H-Unit classroom held over a dozen wood-veneered office tables (manufactured by Prison Industries, one of SQ's few profit centers) with a plethora of chairs. A blue-shirted inmate clerk pushing a broom around the room reminded us to put the chairs back up on the tables where they belonged, and to restore the room's original configuration after we were done.

"Otherwise the anger management teacher gets *really* pissed off . . ."

Our classroom looked fairly typical. It reminded us how much the public school environment resembles state correctional facilities: inmates and kids, neither wanting to be incarcerated, yet herded through the system, categorized and self-segregated by age and race, while fed substandard daily grub. There is very little difference.

The classroom walls were adorned with slogans and sayings heralding respect, honesty, and responsibility. The ten Bill of Rights were tacked across the top of the big whiteboard on the main wall—as if convicts enjoy certain unalienable rights while being locked up. Once you hit San Quentin, you check your Bill of Rights at the door.

There was a color portrait of a passive-looking, shirtless black man with his infant son lying on his chest—graphic support for the fatherhood/parenting class. Next to that was a wild-eyed portrait of Frida Kahlo, though with her bushy eyebrows and a daisy stuck in her hair, poor Frida looked more like a Puerto Rican prison tranny than an esteemed Mexican painter.

Twenty minutes dragged by after we were announced. We anticipated our first horde of motivated wannabe scribes crossing the yard to be part of the Z'men's maiden voyage of "Finding Your Voice on the Page." At nearly seven o'clock we were still nervously waiting for the room to fill up.

It didn't.

A trio of blue-shirted inmates modestly made their entrance through the front door. Jeez. Our preliminary roll sheet showed ten pre-registered names. Crestfallen, we harkened back to our music biz days when John-Cougar-before-he-was-John-Mellencamp and his mighty six-piece band, the Zone, had played a San Francisco nightclub back in 1979. His record label, Mercury/PolyGram, had "papered" the house that night, but could only manage about forty people. Terrific. Welcome to the John Cougar version of Creative Writing at San Quentin. This was H-Unit, for Christ's sake. A freaking prison! It wasn't as if these guys had anyplace better to be. Mandatory classroom attendance? Not quite.

We eyeballed our three students, awkwardly clustered around a single table, and cleared the rest of the furniture to create a wider, more open classroom environment. We handed each guy a plastic pen and a white, lined legal-sized pad (not yellow, so as to avoid the legalese vibe). Each inmate was dressed in baggy, ill-fitting denim pants and a blue smock top with a bold yellow "CDCR" (California Department of Corrections and Rehabilitation) emblazoned on the back. Nobody was particularly scary-looking. Of course we were unarmed except for the required whistle that hung around our necks. Any trouble, after three blasts of the whistle the CO's would come running. We hoped. We nervously shook hands with each student as we introduced ourselves: Hello Delonte, a mild-mannered and fresh-faced twenty-something African American from Compton. Hello, Raymond M., a white redneck peckerwood with an engineer's cap perched on the back of his head and three days of growth on his face. And a Latino in his early thirties introduced himself as Doug the Poet.

"You guys teach poetry?"

"Nope," said Kent dismissively, pissed off and disappointed.

"We don't, actually," Keith explained more diplomatically. "Poetry is a completely different animal from nonfiction. Sorry, man."

Doug eyed the door, but stuck around, at least for the next hour until smoke break.

"I'm already taking a writing class up on the hill," said Raymond, pointing outside, covering his ass in case he too decided to bail next week. "It's goin' pretty good, but I figured I'd come see what you guys are up to."

Suddenly the classroom door swung open and two more white males entered, vociferously engaged in conversation. It was an entrance right out of *Rio Bravo* meets *The Shawshank Redemption*.

"Is this the Creative Writing class?" one of the fellas asked matter-of-factly. They both surveyed the vacant room, not particularly bothered by the lack of numbers.

"Grab a chair, guys," we said in unison.

"You guys twins?" smiled the taller lanky inmate with a Brooklyn brogue. He stuck out his hand. "Colm. And this here is my buddy Norton. You need to see our ID's?"

"Naw, we trust you," said Keith. "Grab a seat and sign in, we're just getting started."

"So-so-so-so-so you-you guys wr-wr-wrote a book with the Hells Angels? No shit?" Norton blurted a hurried stutter, a frazzled meth casualty.

"Yeah, no shit," said Kent. "We'll fill you in."

"So . . . "—long pause—"you interested in writing?" asked Keith, "'Cause we wanna put a little different slant on this class—"

"Little background first," added Kent. "We started writing books in 1990, and got published in '94. Our philosophy: If we can do it, anybody can. We've been living off the blank page, full-time, since August 2001. Can't say I recommend it, but you can expect this to be a pretty hands-on class. What we want from you is some edge in the writing. Give us something real!"

"To be honest," continued Keith, "we want to see if this teaching thing works for us."

"So, why are you guys really here?" asked Delonte, cutting to the chase. "You lookin' for material?"

We both smiled. Prison is about brass tacks, the bottom line.

"Here's what's in it for us," Kent responded. "Help us get through our week and we'll help you get through yours."

"Just so you know, we could be instructing a college extension course and gettin' paid," said Keith. "But it ain't about that. Friday is the end of our work week, and we need inspiration, too. We're two guys cooped up in a room all day—kinda like you. When we're not at home, we're out on the road somewhere, living in a Howard Johnson's. Teaching here seemed like a better idea than dicking around with a bunch of green college kids and bored lawyers, accountants, and wannabe novelists."

Delonte nodded his head. Our first hurdle, cleared.

Word of warning, The Z'men's rap closely resembled watching a Wimbledon tennis match. Heads swiveled back and forth, amused, listening to our alternating spiel.

"You'll get as much out of this class as you put into it," Keith said. "Writing with a regular regimen is like working out in the gym. No pain, no gain. The more you write, the stronger your stuff gets and the easier it is to find your voice on the page."

"Writing is different these days," finished Kent. "While people don't write letters so much, except you guys, they e-mail and blog. Whether you're writing to your peeps at home or e-mailing on the outside, you'll need to find the direct link between what's in your head and what makes it onto the page. We wanna take out the middle man."

"Everybody on this yard has to have exciting stories to share, otherwise, how the hell did you get here?" asked Keith. "Plus, we promise not to get too bogged down with grammar, punctuation, and syntax."

"A sin tax?" asked Norton.

"Syntax. It's how a sentence is structured," replied Kent. "Anyway, let's not trip about that stuff. Each Friday we'll give you a short lesson on writing—you know, important stuff, basic rules, like 'Show Don't Tell.' Don't just tell us. Show us. Paint us a picture with words."

The inmates exchanged blank stares.

"Here's the bargain," said Keith. "We let you into our world. You let us into yours. We tell you what's happening with the books

we're working on. We just put out a thriller novel with William Mor-
row/HarperCollins called *Dead in 5 Heartbeats*. And right now, we're
talking about working with Adam and Jamie from the *Mythbusters*
show on the Discovery Channel. Anybody heard of them?"

Blank stares all around. Contrary to law and order proselytizers,
no extensive cable TV packages get piped into Q.

"Okay, then our latest biography on Huey P. Newton is currently in production. Our first publisher fired our asses, but we got
picked up by another house anyway. We'll tell you how that went
down. Stuff like that."

A smile crossed Delonte's face. "Huey Newton, the Black
Panther?"

Kent nodded affirmatively. "Look guys, we promise we'll give
you the straight shit on writing. When cover art arrives for a book,
we'll bring it in. You tell us whether it grabs you or not. If our
editor is an asshole, you'll hear about it. If she's cool, you'll know
firsthand. You'll see what a first-pass manuscript looks like. We can
talk about money advances and film rights. We'll explain how the
funds get doled out since publishers assume that most authors are
unreliable flakes and drunks, so they purposely hand out the money
in installments. Bet'cha didn't know that."

"But remember, this isn't about us," said Keith. "We help you
find your own voices. At the very least, you'll become a better letter-
writer or at least better able to coax your parole board to get you the
hell outta this place."

"We're not recruiting the next Eddie Bunker, and the warden's office doesn't want us coming here in search of the next
Eldridge Cleaver or Mumia Abu-Jamal," said Kent. "But we can
show you how to organize a book proposal to try and sell yourself as an author once you get released."

"And one more thing," said Keith, ending the discussion, "Let's
demystify the whole writing thing. Writing is for everybody. Our job
is to get you guys hooked . . . on coming here every Friday."

Our small quorum, hands-on experts at addiction, nodded at the final point.

Keith turned around and scrawled a large message up on the board.

"WRITERS TAKE TOURS OF OTHER PEOPLE'S LIVES."

"And remember," Keith said, "whatever you choose to write inside these walls, fiction, truthfulness, and anonymity are always the options."

Kent writes a dueling message up on the other board.

"WRITERS ARE PAID LIARS AND PROFESSIONAL BULLSHIT ARTISTS, JUST LIKE CRIMINALS."

"Okay. Let's take a quick tour and do some writing," said Kent, clapping his hands. "Give us a little slice of life. H-Unit style. Something off the top of your heads. Ready? Set? Go!"

We grabbed a couple of chairs and sat down, arms folded, while our small contingent began scribbling away. After twenty-five minutes, each student slapped down a finished assignment.

Keith picked up Raymond's paper. "You wanna read what you wrote?" He shook his head. The thought of standing in front of five guys terrified Raymond.

"Okay, uh, mind if I read it?" Keith asked.

Raymond shrugged. "It's not very good."

Keith straightened out the page and read aloud.

Fresh off the bus, endorsed from Tracy, out of orange and straight into blues, I'm assigned to a cell in North Block with a dozen other inmates. As I turn, all I see is some poor bastard getting two quick jabs with a right. He falls to the ground. Then a powerful blow, a knee to the nose. Watching the blood flow from his face, I stand there in a daze as the sirens blare. I see the CO's slapping the cuffs on the dude still standing. He yells as he's being dragged away. My head echoes his words, 'Welcome to the yard, fish.'

"Fish" is a term for a prison tenderfoot. Pretty tough stuff. Hardly what you'd read at a Stanford Continuing Education class.

Hearing Ray's words read aloud gave Colm confidence.

"Here, read mine."

> Concrete, steel, dust, and dirt. Where's the inspiration? F**k the inspiration. Just write. Get a flow going. See what you got in you. Be creative. It's called creative writing, right? See where your creativity lies. Put some words on the page and let the pen do the work. Let the words take you away to another place or another time because anyplace at all is better than this place or worse. Just write and get the f**k out of here for a while. Let that be the inspiration.

In one quick burst, Colm had stumbled onto something key. An epiphany. The mission of our class. These five guys, losers at first glance, were keeping up their ends of the bargain. Now we needed to keep up ours. It was time to spread the word and get more butts in the seats.

CHAPTER 6

The Power of the ReadBack

Education classes for H-Unit's Success Program operated on a quarterly basis as opposed to semesters. We promised, barring any unforeseen cross-country road trips, that we would hold at least nine classes of "Finding Your Voice on the Page" per quarter. We managed to hold on to our core of five pupils after that maiden voyage class on April 11, 2003. Delonte, Ray, Norton, Colm, and Doug the Poet hung on and returned for Week Number Two. Over the next few weeks, word spread throughout the dorms and on the yard about "this new thing" on Friday nights. One evening during that first year, a muscular, tanned guy in his late twenties approached us before class. We could tell he was a "repeat offender" by his penitentiary shuffle—shoulders thrown back while strolling with brazen authority. (A lot of outlaw bike-riders walk like that too.) He was shorter than us, stocky and built close to the ground like a fireplug. He introduced himself, rather appropriately, as Rhino.

"You guys wrote that book with Sonny?"

"That's right," Keith affirmed, and stuck out his hand. "Keith Z. Say hello to my bro' Kent."

We shook hands as "Rhino" eyeballed us.

"I know a lot of the club guys in San Jose . . . " He rattled off a few colorful nicknames.

"We mostly hung out with Oakland and Arizona guys. You a bike rider?"

"Sure am," Rhino responded smugly.

"Figured as much." The stroll gives 'em away every time. "What do you ride?"

Rhino's eyes lit up. It was as if we were asking him about his kids.

"I got a retro seventies bike, '77 Harley XLCR1000 with a V-twin engine, 998 cc's. It's fairly stock except for a Springer front end. A racer, not a cruiser."

"Pre-AMC?"

"Abso-f**kin'-lutely. My old lady rides a 1995 883, a Sportster that I rebuilt after she stacked it. We do the run to Street Vibrations up in Reno. You guys ride?"

"No, we don't." We've never bullshitted anybody about the fact that we don't ride motorcycles, and that we drive roadsters instead. Rhino was undaunted. After we dropped a few names we knew, he cracked a smile, apparently convinced of our earnestness.

"What is this class again?"

"Creative Writing: Finding Your Voice on the Page."

"I don't write worth shit. Mind if I sit in?"

"Mi casa, su casa," Kent said, imitating Lance the Junkie, the *Pulp Fiction* movie character played by Eric Stoltz.

We gradually picked up a couple more newbies in addition to Rhino, building our roster more slowly than we'd originally envisioned. One was a guy who called himself Marlowe, a grizzled, pale-skinned, and silver-haired fellow in his late sixties. He wrote a smashing piece about Greenwich Village circa 1964, partly pilfered from Hemingway.

McDougal Street in the sixties was a movable feast. The sidewalks were so crowded you often had to walk and lounge in the street. I guess in my mind's eye, I can go there still, just by watching that old Howard Koch movie, *The President's Analyst*, where a lot of the scenes were filmed. In the summer, the Village was like an outdoor market. It held the mystery and wild promise in the world. My first hero I ran into was Shel Silverstein. He had a little pad over on Prince Street and could often be seen in the Kettle of Fish.

Everybody could see that Marlowe was a sophisticate and a well-read cat, and rather than put him down as a silly old git, the other class members gave him due respect.

Another newbie, Cazale, was a decent enough chap. According to Cazale, he was a veteran of the first Iraq war. We grimaced a little when we spotted a few tattoos on his right shoulder that signified white power. While it made us a little uncomfortable, we didn't bring it up. Two more new guys showed up, apparently buddies serving their time together, just like Norton and Colm. A dark, curly-haired fellow signed the all-important roving attendance sheet, which was how we kept track of classroom attendance. The name "King James" was scrawled right next to a CDC number and bunk address—4H, 22 Up (translated roughly: dorm #4, upper bunk #22). We later found out that the King was a successful club deejay in San Francisco's South of Market area. He got popped for selling enough E tablets to catch a serious drug-dealing beef. His friend Moz was a handsome long-haired Pacific Islander with a little Japanese blood in him. Moz and King James were a couple of nightclub hip dogs to be sure—incarcerated to keep consensual adult society safe from the "insidious scourge" of designer nightclub drugs.

With a few more SQ Fridays under our belts (and no negative feedback from the home front), the general personality and routine of the class took shape. We adapted custom writing topics to keep the guys hooked and interested. Stuff like "Funny Where Life Takes You" or "The Last Time I Saw _____," which was inspired by a sad and regretful excerpt Kent read aloud from Jack Kerouac's *On the*

Road about the last time Sal Paradise sees Dean Moriarty on the streets of Manhattan. The writing was already so visceral and gutsy, we didn't know how much further we could push these guys. Sometimes when things got too intense, we would pull back and revert to more introspective topics—subjects like "Time to Go Inward" (based on the lyrics of a tune by Rodney Crowell) or "A Personal Moment of Tranquility."

Within the first few classroom sessions, we stumbled upon a technique of how best to evaluate and highlight a student's in-class writing. We had discovered that the more interactive and participatory the class became, the better we could hold the students' interest. So we invented something we called "the ReadBack." The ReadBack quickly turned into the cornerstone method of how we taught our class, and how we might accelerate our students' literary skills. Rather than "grade" or rewrite each paper with cogent and specific comments relating to their writing, the ReadBack simply consisted of typing up everybody's in-class hand-scrawled writing assignment into one large Word document, then printing up copies of the document and passing them out. Rather than the students' stumbling through reciting their own stuff, we (Kent and Keith) took turns reading each person's contribution while everyone followed along on their own personal copies of everybody's writings.

One of the primary benefits of the ReadBack was that each student, by following along word for word as we read through nearly six thousand words of copy, was able view the structure of each piece. Also, their reading comprehension skills were tested in the process of reading along. Without a hard copy to read along to, the concept of the ReadBack would have been doomed from the start. But with the hard copy, 95 percent of the students had no problem following along. In fact, there was a certain tension in the room as each student anticipated hearing their passage read aloud. Nobody got bored.

We added a little "mustard" to our readings of the narratives, which quickened the pace of the ReadBack and also produced immediate reactions from the class. Some pretty hard-hitting prose drew lots of ooh's and aah's and laughs, as well as shock and awe over the quality of the stories that leapt from the pages. After a few dramatized readings of hilarious car chases with the cops or heart-rending portraits of ex-wives and children witnessing daddy's arrest, or angst-ridden tales of a drunken mom or dad, the most common response was:

"Damn! Did we write that stuff?"

"Trust us," we'd tell them, "We did a little light line editing and spell checking. Other than that, what you're hearin' is what we're gettin'."

Some passages during the ReadBack were so potent they would draw spontaneous noisy applause from the class. We watched racial barriers blown to bits as blacks applauded Mexicans who, for the first time, could relate to whitey having the same drunken parents as they'd grown up with in the barrio. Quite often a writer whose work was being cheered wouldn't quite know how to handle such a response from his peers. Usually, he would keep his head down, half embarrassed, or look straight ahead and quietly take it in. All week long these men were herded and ordered around, bound by mind-numbing routine. Suddenly, they were being praised for something they had created. Right away it was apparent that most of these H-Unit inmate-types weren't accustomed to being singled out and recognized for producing quality original work.

After the first few ReadBacks, we needed a way to keep track of the writings and archive them. Guys started asking for extra copies to send back to family and friends on the outside. Soon our typed-up assignments transformed into an ongoing anthology/newsletter, a written record of each class output. Our tidy little document needed a name, so the following week, we threw around a few suggestions, something to do with "hard times" out on the yard.

A Mexican inmate, Señor Spanky, spoke out. "Sure it's hard time, but it's our time."

That was it! *Yard Time, Hard Time, Our Time.* The name stuck.

One night as we packed up our gear and said our goodbyes to the lingering students—guys who liked to hang out and talk about books and rock 'n' roll, just for some basic outside civilian interaction—we walked outside towards the sally port gate to get buzzed out of the H-Unit yard.

An inmate approached us from behind. Actually, we felt his massive shadow before we saw him. He was over 300 pounds, with arms completely covered in punk rock tats. His floppy, half-buttoned blue chambray work shirt exposed many more Gothic body ink images etched around his bulbous chest.

"Are you those guys teaching the writing class?"

"That would be us," we said in unison.

"Steve Ramone." He stuck out his fleshy oversized paw.

"What can we do for you, Mr. Ramone?" We liked referring to prisoners as "Mr." It had an ironic ring to it.

"Got any more room in your class?"

"Just show up next week. Six-thirty, right after chow. You can 'audit' the class one time. If you like it, you can—"

"No, I definitely wanna sign up. I love to write, and I've heard good things about you guys. Are you into fantasy and horror?"

"Not really. But one of our main influences is Harlan Ellison. Ever heard of him?"

"Demon with the Glass Hand?"

"That's the guy."

We watched the wheels spin inside Ramone's head. "I'll see you next Friday."

On the drive back home to Oakland from Marin County (via the Richmond-San Rafael Bridge), we blew in a call to our father, Joe, with an update. He was awaiting our call. We told him we were making slow but sure progress, that the class had gone into double-digits, closing in on the teens—lucky thirteen students to be exact. We told him how the guys broke into applause when we read their stuff out loud back to them. Joe was touched and pleased with our modest progress. We could tell we were living out his unfulfilled dream.

"You boys are doing the right thing. Stay with it."

"Thanks, Joe." (We've always referred to our father by his first name since we were teenagers.)

Our conversation in the car on the way home drifted to what an inmate had told Kent after class. It had to do with another Success Program course.

"You know the guy who teaches yoga and meditation every week?" said Kent.

"Yeah, he's a great guy. How's his class doing?" Keith replied.

"Evidently he's got a whole bunch of guys doing yoga exercises every week."

"Really?"

"According to one of our guys, one of the shot-callers on the yard decided to take his yoga class."

(Each race has designated "shot-callers" out on any prison yard. If any beefs or conflicts occur between the races—blacks, whites, Mexicans, and "others"—rather than fighting it out individually, the shot-callers intervene and mete out justice. It's part of the organized underground system of prison justice. Just exactly who is and isn't a shot-caller, nobody knows for sure.)

"Anyway," continued Kent, "when the shot-caller guy enrolled in the yoga class, all of a sudden it became way cool to do stretching and meditation."

"Wow. We need something like that to happen to us, something to spike our attendance."

That Saturday night, Keith and his wife Gladys were propped up against the bar enjoying a pint or three at the Edinburgh Castle, a longtime public house on Geary Boulevard, located in the center of San Francisco's dicey Tenderloin district. "The Castle" is a lively literary hangout for many Bay Area writer types, including Alan Black, the head barman, novelist, and general manager of the vaulted British-American pub, whose reputation had spread worldwide. The place is well known for hosting many celebrated book and reading events by such famous prize-winning British and American writers as Irvine Welsh, the respected Scottish author of *Trainspotting.* Black himself is a pretty rad journalist and author. Keeping another busy Saturday night under control, Alan shoved two brimming pints of Newcastle Brown Ale toward us.

"What's the word, Alan?" Keith asked.

"We're doing a reading next month. I'm making up the flyers and postcards right now," said Alan. "We're featuring two writers who did time in the pen. One guy did twelve years in Sing Sing, and the other spent time locked down in a gulag in Russia."

"Get outta here," Keith said, as a lightbulb went off in his head. "Alan, you know Kent and I started teaching a creative writing class inside San Quentin."

"No kidding," Alan said, grinning.

"And we got some pretty decent writers. What if we could feature the writing by our guys, who are actually bunked up in San Quentin as we speak?"

"I like where you're going with this."

"Just give me the opening slot. Ten minutes. Whaddya say?"

"Let's do it," said Alan decisively. "Oh, and by the way, it's gonna be broadcast on KALW, the local noncommercial community radio station."

"Even better," Keith replied, as the two shook on it. It would be our class's media debut!

The next Friday we opened the class with the announcement. "How would you guys like to have your stuff read at a literary event in San Francisco? And get this: it'll be broadcast on the radio."

A buzz circulated through the classroom.

"A friend of ours books cutting-edge literary events at the Edinburgh Castle in San Francisco. He's headlining a couple of authors who did time in prison, so I went ahead and volunteered you guys to open the show by me reading some of your writing."

One thing we'd already learned about being around incarcerated inmates: for every thumbs-up reaction you get, there's a few cynical and pessimistic reactions on the other side. This time it came from one of the veteran cons.

"You know, you'll need to clear this through the warden's office—and I doubt that will happen. You guys could catch shit if you do this without permission."

"So we'll just get permission."

"Good luck with that," Delonte from Compton piped in.

"Leave that to us. You guys just concentrate on writing. Here's the topic: Let's keep it simple. Yard Time, Hard Time, Our Time. Let's just write about that."

The next Monday we called Jean Bracy from the Education Department and explained our situation. Ms. Bracy suggested we submit the finished writing for her to pass on directly to Warden Jeanne Woodford's office to gain proper clearance. We attached a succinct letter to the writing, explaining that it would be a public reading and radio broadcast. The fuse was lit, and we hoped for the best.

Two days before the Saturday affair at the Castle, we received clearance for our *Yard Time, Hard Time, Our Time* reading. Warden Woodford personally read through the gritty prose, which detailed the realities on the yard, good and bad, ugly and not so ugly. Upon closer inspection we saw that two pieces—vigorous diatribes by Colm and Norton generously peppered with loads of f-bombs— had been crossed out and banished.

We faced the men that Friday, the next day, not sure how to break the news.

"Listen guys, we got good news and bad news."

A wave of expected disappointment rippled through the room.

Keith began: "First of all, the reading is on. We got clearance from the warden. Unfortunately, two pieces by Norton and Colm have been deleted. Frankly, we don't know exactly how to react to this."

Then Kent continued: "I think the best thing would be to discuss this amongst ourselves, and in the end we can take a vote as to whether or not you guys would like us to go through with this. If you choose all or nothing and cancel our participation in the reading, we understand. No hard feelings. It's up to you guys."

As a few opinions were bantered about, before the discussion gathered too much momentum, Norton raised his hand. "L-l-l-look," he said in his yard-time stutter, "I'll withdraw my writing if it m-m-means that we can still do this."

Colm joined in. "Me too. We'll gladly step aside so that everybody else can be part of the reading. It's okay with us. Go for it."

A hush permeated the room. Heads nodded. The reading was on.

We were genuinely touched by Norton and Colm's gesture.

After lights out that Saturday night at the Q, a wave of San Quentin convicts plugged in their FM headphones and listened to their brothers bear their literary souls over Northern California airwaves. Just like the wild ducks and pigeons who flew in and out of the H-Unit grounds with impunity, here was the debut of "Finding Your Voice on the Page," leaving the confines of the yard and the little cinder block classroom, beaming across Bay Area skies.

The reading marked the debut of a handful of writers, including Steve Ramone, who touched on the theme of lost freedom.

I saw a seagull once, tattered wings torn by concertina wire, ravaged veteran of the San Quentin sky wars, charge down and slash open a paper lunch sack, extract peanut butter, and trade it on the yard for a cigarette. It wasn't the same gull who had just shit on me, but I understood their message.

They were free.

Free not to do hard time for f**king up.

To the gull, they only existed for life and death, the quintessential arbitrators of the animal kingdom.

No prisons exist for killer whales who bash baby seals to death for fun, no courts for chicken-stealing foxes, jewel-thieving ferrets, and crocodiles who eat their young.

Yin and Yang.

The cycle of life.

I heard a sparrow once sing like a cell phone.

I wonder if he was calling for bail.

By July 2003 we had completed our first quarter. We had made it through our first barrier: ten complete classes! We had also managed to break past a dozen enrollees. We hadn't washed out after six weeks, as was previously prognosticated that first week by the CO with the giant ring of keys. We were still standing! For the price of a couple of dozen legal tablets of paper and some cheap plastic PaperMate pens, we had something real to strive for other than our own self-centered goals as professional writers and published authors. The Inner Void was being filled.

Once the first quarter ended, we stopped by an office supply store the morning of the class. We purchased a box of gold parchment paper, a package of embossed gold seals, and some cheap, funky Print Shop computer software. We sorted through the generic graphics, made some selections, and created our first customized amber-colored parchment certificate. We'd picked out a corny ornate border and had also found a drawing of an old-fashioned typewriter under which we typed out the class name, "Finding Your Voice on the Page." Beneath that, we inserted the banner line, "In Recognition of Outstanding Achievement" with a large space reserved for each student's name to be typed in caps, using a flashy, elaborate font. Beneath the name space was large block letters that proclaimed, "CERTIFICATE OF COMPLETION." At the very bottom we left space for our names and signatures. We signed and numbered each one of our graphic creations. Two journeymen writers—us!—suddenly felt like literary legends. The certificate was resplendent in hues of bright green, brown, blue, purple, and orange. Upon each certificate, we planted a shiny embossed circular gold seal and an American flag sticker next to each name.

We made a big deal out of handing out each certificate—a few "atta boy's" and some "job-well-done's." We talked about each student's work, congratulated them heartily, and invited them to register for the next quarter.

Our first inclination was that the certificates were a bit too gaudy and a little cheesy, too.

Wrong.

You couldn't wipe the smiles off the faces of these guys with a wire brush as each "writer" admired the parchment documents we handed out. Gold-sealed, homemade certificates came to represent another strange currency behind prison walls. They would eventually be collected from quarter to quarter, sent off to mothers, wives, and significant others, and shown to parole officers, proof that these men were making the effort to change and that one day they would be released back into the real world and into the arms of loved ones and families.

CHAPTER 7

Layabouts and Lowlifes

San Quentin and our new H-Unit writing class impacted us on the social front in the civilian/outside world. It wasn't long before two compelling forces—SQ and the "Finding Your Voice on the Page" class—shook our private lives. We were like brand-new parents turned braggarts, sharing the hard-edged writing that was coming out of the cinder block classroom. After spending time around authors brandishing what they imagined to be vivid, violent prose, these guys, albeit unpolished, were the real deal.

Even though we were following up a bestseller, *Hell's Angel,* and working with creative people like the team on television's *Mythbusters,* the Friday class complemented our own writing priorities and became an important spoke in the wheel of our literary universe. Pity our friends and family who had to put up with our ravings about the prose we were harvesting. We were buzzed about its progress. The students took guidance well, and had a ton of questions about writing and the publishing world. The energy level was much more kinetic and the curiosity level higher than in standard low-key college classes and timid evening creative writing workshops. Classroom participation and Q&A were spirited. Guys raised their hands and nearly jumped out of their chairs for the chance to speak. The learning process fascinated them, almost in a childlike way. For example, one time we constructed a three-act thriller tale on the dry board to illustrate what elements go into the three-act structure (character introduction, setting, conflict, reaction, climax, resolution, etc.) of a typical storyline. We devised a Hitchcock-type plot about a stranger picking up the wrong contraband suitcase in the airport. The idea of constructing their own tight story lines jolted the men's enthusiasm.

The class vibe was anything but subdued. At times the discussion and our ReadBacks grew so boisterous that a CO would poke his or her head into the small front door window just to check up on things. Yet the cops left us alone. They never came in and sat in on the class, nor did they approach us afterwards with questions or comments. We were given great latitude.

Through class discussion, we got a peek into the loneliness and frustrations of doing time in state, county, and federal institutions. Many times guys came up after class with the desire to write their memoirs. What better place to begin than while sitting in jail with nothing but time on their hands while getting three square meals? A three-act story arc helped them visualize their own stories clearly.

We had learned early on during our training not to ask about an inmate's crime. Honestly, we didn't care. So we made it our policy not to discuss an inmate's transgressions unless they brought it up themselves. If they wished to tell us, fine. Otherwise, unless something came up in their writing, with the vast majority of our students, we had no idea what they were inside for. That only made it easier for us to be nonjudgmental and keep an emotional distance.

More than anything the short-timers' convictions were usually related to dope, meth, and pot—with some violent crime thrown in. We didn't perceive each student by his misdeeds. It wasn't as if we thought, well there's a burglar over by the door, a drug dealer sitting up front, and a bank robber in the back row. Most were zany personalities that central casting couldn't have possibly come up with—

a crew of all races: black, whites, Sureños and Norteños (Southern and Northern Mexicans), original gangsters (or OGs), hip-hoppers, "others" (the Asians, Native Americans, and Pacific Islanders). Outside of a few scary-looking, tattooed tough dudes with awful dental work, these were people most of us would walk past on the streets and not think twice about.

We maintained a fairly strict teacher-student relationship with the guys. We were taught during brown card instruction to avoid taking sides for or against the authority system that was firmly in place at H-Unit. Our goal every Friday night was to turn that drab cinder block classroom into a bustling writing factory filled with guys who'd never imagined themselves skillfully wielding words and putting thoughts into cohesively written first- and third-person narratives.

If you surveyed the room, you would see men of all shapes, sizes, colors, and levels of education. Some were skinny and reedy; others blocked out the sky. Most had barely scraped through high school. Many were claimed by the street before education took root. Some came with a few semesters of junior college, while even fewer (the stoners) had earned bachelor's degrees. A few were schooled in the finery of drug cooking and cannabis horticulture in the wilds of California's Humboldt and Lake Counties. We'd been led to believe that we would inherit a crew of thickos and dolts who could barely complete a sentence. Yet even the slower, stultified, learning-impaired students that we had were carried by the rest of the group. They learned and improved a great deal individually, and didn't slow down our progress as a class. We saw more encouragement than competition among the classmates.

Personalities quickly emerged, particularly those of the leaders. A sizable chunk of the inmates in our classes was at Q courtesy of the meth "culture." (Let it be known! Meth is the true scourge of America!) Eddie was an impish street urchin who expressed himself with clever color-inked cartoons and doggerel poetry. "Midget Porn" was a tweaker who manufactured his own line of custom bawdy greeting cards cut from discarded manila folders. MP sat on the floor by the front of the class, instead of at a desk, during ReadBacks.

San Quentin had become the damnedest place. You didn't know who might drop in. Since many (mostly white) H-Unit inmates watched NASCAR on Saturdays, the former NFL Washington Redskins coach Joe Gibbs from Joe Gibbs Racing visited the yard with one of his racing cars—to the inmates' delight—and spoke to them about Christianity. During the first weeks after we set up shop in 2003, Metallica shot one of their videos, "St. Anger," live in front of one of the North Block tiers and outdoors on another open yard, no stage, in front of an audience of orange-clad inmates separated from the band only by a line of armed CO's. We were bummed when we found out after the fact that as brown card holders we could have joined the crowd and watched the show. Staging Metallica live at Q is an example of how media-savvy the prison can be in comparison to most other prisons throughout the world.

Teaching wasn't that tough of a craft to master. Our mission became basic: turn a roomful of inmates into writers in only a matter of a few classes, getting them up and writing quickly. No strenuous prerequisite lectures. Simply discuss a few writing tips and then pass out the cheap plastic pens (no metal clips) and paper (legal tablets, no wire-bound notebooks) so they could apply what they'd learned and have at it! But first we had to redefine the meaning of "writer" to signify not just published authors, journalists, essayists, or poets, but something broader, continuing to demystify the perception of who and what a writer is. We hoped to open the guys' imaginations by showing them how easily they could communicate through the written word without getting mired in preconceptions and academic barriers. We proselytized that writing was no big secret, no big deal, and that all one had to do was open a direct pipeline between your thoughts and what you scrawl onto the paper. That alone makes you a writer, and that was our prime objective.

It only took a couple of quarters for the class to catch on as word traveled around the prison yard about the goofy twin writers who finished each other's sentences, who had written books with bikers and had worked with Johnny Rotten, and who—most importantly!—gave out free pens and paper. Despite previous and modest successes writing bestsellers and fleshing out other peoples' lives on paper for a living, we were experiencing a far different high. Hmm, we thought, so this is what attracts folks to become teachers despite the lousy pay and the anti-intellectual sentiment of many Americans. Very interesting!

Soon each Friday night after teaching our class, during the nearly one-mile trudge from H-Unit back to the front East Gate, we felt rejuvenated by this awful place, San Quentin. "Finding Your Voice on the Page" was a little like living inside some of our favorite movies, motion pictures like *Stand and Deliver* and *Dead Poets Society* with a dash of TV's *Welcome Back, Kotter*, all rolled into one. Friday night with a bunch of jailbirds rocked our world. Hallelujah!

As we walked back to the car, we would often flash back to the elder veteran volunteers we'd met during the state training sessions, people who had been coming inside this terrible place for ten or twenty years. Had we been bitten by the same bug that kept these people returning year after year?

There ought to be a special place in heaven for all wives of identical twins, but especially for ours, who are willing to give up Friday nights without a complaint. It was Russian TV commentator Vladimir Posner (whom we once booked as a *Gavin* convention keynote speaker) who remarked at the extreme differences between the women in our lives. One blonde, Keith's wife, Gladys, from Scotland, and one brunette, Kent's spouse, Deborah, from Southern California. Not only do they put up (and compete) with the closeness of two crazed brothers who finish each other's sentences and write together ten hours a day, but since our writing careers began, our wives have had to act as anchors as we navigate the choppy waters of meeting writing and print deadlines, creating book ideas, and crafting pitches and proposals from scratch. Not a day goes by when we're not thankful for our wives, who have tolerated the bizarre parade of subject matters we've dragged into our households: books on Hell's Angels, the Black Panthers, Chicago mobsters, the Sex Pistols, and shock rockers. As our eighty-something-year-old mother once asked, "Can't you boys write about nice people?" And on top of everything else, now there's prison every Friday night? Gawd only knows how the families of *full-time* prison staffers and correction officers contend with it.

Prison is a voyeuristic subject matter that rivets millions of television viewers, especially those who have never had a friend, relative, or loved one who has had to fight the criminal justice system, post a bail bond, or do hard time. Over the past decade, our society has changed, as the possibility of being thrown in the pen is no longer inconceivable, whether it's to the white- or blue-collar, middle- or working-class people of America. (Poor folks already know the drill.) If we have a society that unflinchingly jails troublemakers like Martha Stewart, Lindsay Lohan, and Paris Hilton (ironically, all females!), couldn't anybody's ass be up for grabs? Aside from the many privileged Wall Street banksters, corporate power brokers, and insider-trading politicians who routinely escape criminal prosecution, there's hardly anybody in America who isn't just a handcuff click, false accusation, or buzz-driving offense away from jail. In a nation of equal opportunity jailors, step too far out of line and somebody lowers the boom. We thrive on *schadenfreude*—pleasure derived from the misfortune of others—which is broadcast daily into the homes of millions by our 24-hour cable news cycle. If we as a society operate under the auspices of "zero tolerance," and if Martha, Paris, and Lindsay are easy pickings for incarceration, how hard can it be for America's poor and "criminal class" to end up in the clutches of jail with inflated charges? Not too difficult.

That said, nothing about prison culture impressed us or influenced us to become hug-a-thugs, quasi-criminals, or apologists for the inmates. Quite the contrary; we feel that chances are most, if not all, of our students deserve at least some level of punishment. It's difficult to end up in prison by being completely innocent. But the racial divisiveness that pervades a prison yard is not a pretty sight: it's petty, socially prehistoric, passé, and outdated.

Turning on the TV, you'll quickly find there's no escaping prison culture overload. Flick on the cable television networks and you'll see popular "lockdown" show marathons. In feeding America's frenzy for incarceration, many of the unscripted reality series project stereotypes of both correctional officers and inmates. Most of the faces we see on the lockdown shows bear little resemblance, outside of their state-issued clothing, to the guys writing in our class. And despite the public's fascination with anti-heroes and bad boys, the general public nationwide views criminals and inmates with incredible disdain. In supposedly liberal newspapers such as the *San Francisco Chronicle*, online reader comments to prison stories about inmate crowding, hunger strikes, and substandard medical care are usually vicious and blatantly unsympathetic. What *has* changed is the public's tolerance towards spending money jailing and warehousing the nonviolent and the drug offenders. Only in the age of recession and state and county budget crisis is public opinion shifting. Even ultra-conservative groups might not prefer strict punishment and long third-strike sentences for nonviolent offenders over more fiscally sensible solutions.

While executions are viewed as "closure" for victims' families, Three Strikes Laws and stringent sentencing regulations are being called into question across the political spectrum, weighed against the financial realities of states and counties having to enforce and enact laws previously championed by ambitious politicians and career-climbing talk show hosts. Waiting in the wings are the private prisons, institutions built and run by corporations and private entities like Corrections Corporation of America (CCA) and the GEO Group, whose shares are publicly traded on the New York Stock Exchange. Luckily there is no love lost between the antiunion corporate prison builders and the correctional officers trade unions; otherwise, that alone could create one rather ominous and unholy alliance. Yet one inmate who actually did time in several CCA establishments vehemently preferred being locked up in a private enterprise prison to serving inside a state-run facility. He claimed the chain of command was much more transparent and efficient.

Looking into the statistics of recidivism, we found California's rate of over 67 percent not that uncommon. We'd already seen recidivism firsthand whenever guys who were released reappeared months or years later on the H-Unit yard. This only hammered home the importance of education as a remedy toward rehabilitation and reduced recidivism. While we've always believed in education, now more than ever we hold an unwavering belief in its power.

As the months passed, one of the most surprising byproducts of our new teaching experience was that rather than feeling overwhelmed and depressed by such a strange and intense environment, we were actually beginning to draw strength and inspiration from it, which seemed neither altogether natural nor healthy. In talking to the other volunteers, we found we weren't alone. Many were, like us, fixing a hole and/or filling a void. One H-Unit volunteer admitted he'd been at it for so long that he was having trouble socializing in the "real world" of civilians and non-felons. That became our first red light warning.

Granted, we were a long way from falling into that trap, but one of the pitfalls we did quickly fall into was that after the first year or so, we'd lost touch with the basic realities and priorities of our friends and peers. Standard dinner party conversation about real estate values, cars, kitchen renovations, and private school for the kids, though extremely important to our friends and family, suddenly seemed vacant and irrelevant to us. Instead of the act of teaching and volunteering enlightening our attitude towards society, making us more understanding and informed, we were growing increasingly thick-skinned, cynical, and at times withdrawn and uncommunicative at social events. This spooked our spouses. After the initial high of teaching came a feeling of distance and isolation around our family and friends.

Our intentions weren't entirely selfless. We were vying for teaching experience in an effort to one day score a shot at academic stability. But the tables had turned, and as much as the inmates seemed to be getting a great deal out of the class, it was changing us even more.

During one holiday dinner party at a friend's house, Chuck, the host, told one of the women guests at the table, "You know, Keith here teaches a creative writing class at San Quentin," to which the woman responded, "Well that's fine for you, but I have absolutely no sympathy for lowlifes and layabouts who get locked up for committing crimes."

"Cool," Keith nodded. "So what is it that you do for a living?"

"I work for the IRS," she replied.

"Really? And what have *you* done to make the world a better place to live, other than auditing other people's tax returns?"

A chilly vibe hovered over the dinner table. Later, the woman's husband, who worked for an academic think tank, mentioned that he had just finished a report that concluded that black Americans were severely disadvantaged within our current educational system and may never catch up.

"So," Keith said, "what happened after you submitted your report?"

"What do you mean?" Think Tank Guy asked, perplexed.

"Did anybody respond? Did anything change?"

"The report went over very well."

"So they paid you to compile a report. What good did it do? How did it change the educational plight for black people in America other than filing a report?"

Keith's wife, Gladys, was angry afterwards. "Doing nice things for disadvantaged people doesn't give you the license to be overbearing, obnoxious, self-righteous, and a self-centered asshole. I feel as if this prison stuff has hardened you.

"I've supported your writing all this time, and a lot of it involves a lot of pretty intense characters. You've worked with punk rockers and biker clubs. Now you're working on a book about the Black Panthers and Huey Newton for God's sake. Then you keep talking about an investigative book on Organized Crime. That's well and fine, but I ask you to do one thing for me."

"What's that?"

"Keep the street out of our home. If you're so concerned about giving convicted felons a better chance in life, fine. I just don't want to see any third-chance losers and lunatics coming around this house."

"Point taken."

Consequently, every time we find ourselves slipping into a tirade of indignation, preaching about warehousing inmates, archaic sentencing laws, or the decriminalization of soft drugs, we are brought back down to earth by our wives, who know better than to allow us to disenfranchise our friends and family. As it turns out, we are the ones living in a self-imposed exile, trapped inside a dream world and Shangri-La of our own making.

CHAPTER 8

Ad Seg and Hot Meds

As the class grew, we experienced distractions and limitations that would drive conventional teachers wacko.

Try to picture teaching a class in this day and age to students with no access to the Internet. At best, prison inmates have limited access to newspapers, magazine subscriptions (which must first pass muster through clogged prison mailroom systems), and network and local news broadcasts on local television, and no extended 24/7 cable news service.

Imagine having to submit every piece of educational media, every movie or television scene on DVD, and every piece of music on CD for administrative scrutiny and approval. Picture showing up to a class and finding out the final prisoner count for the day has delayed your starting time by up to an hour. Or that a specific race is locked down and cannot attend, meaning you carry on without blacks, Mexicans, or whites. Or how about no students at all? Occasionally we'd show up to find the entire prison locked down because of some violence that had occurred on West Block, for example. Programs, meaning classes, are suddenly cancelled. How many teachers deal with classes that are cancelled due to a fog alert?

(A foggy yard is difficult, if not impossible, for the CO's to guard.) So goes the world of prison: a life bogged down in dull routine until something unforeseen happens, and then all hell breaks loose. It's an environment where riots, mass searches, and lockdowns erupt unpredictably. What is particularly frustrating is not being able to properly announce to your students that class is cancelled, having to hope that word trickles out that we haven't flaked but instead, were cut off at the entrance. As a result, we continually cautioned our students that if, for any reason, we were inexplicably absent, we hadn't flaked. We'd been refused entry at the front gate.

A few more things took some getting used to. Like watching the prison ambulance pull up in front of our classroom door, loading in a victim of a stabbing. Or the sound of a buzzer siren alarm followed by the sight of skittish CO's sprinting across the yard, hands on their holsters, with pepper spray, clubs, and other accessories hanging off their belts. The sprint meant that a fracas or some altercation had occurred inside one of the H-Unit dorms. Even stranger was crossing the yard when suddenly an alarm would sound and inmates were required to drop to their knees or sit on the ground while we civilians were expected to keep walking like nothing strange had happened.

Folks often ask if we were scared armed with only paper, ballpoint pens, and a whistle. The answer is, yes, initially we were scared to death, but not so much over the threat of violence. We were more frightened of failure, and that nobody, not even an inmate with endless time on their hands, would bother to show up to our class. Would our lesson plans fly? Could these guys write? Would they find our experiences interesting and valid? Did we have anything relevant to offer to these guys? Perhaps these are universal fears that all teachers share.

Violence was way at the bottom of our list of fears. Very early in the game, in return for our service, we felt an immediate sense of safety inside the classroom. Yes, some of that had to do with the presence of armed guards next door. But mainly, it was because we were essentially locked inside a room full of grateful bodyguards. After writing books with criminals, bike clubs, and mobsters, we had learned that the more transparent your intentions, the better your chances for survival and trust. We adopted such a stance teaching at Quentin. Say what you plan to do and do what you say. Hardly a week goes by when we aren't thanked by inmate students for coming in each Friday and sacrificing our time to teach our weekly course. How many public or private schoolteachers can make that same claim?

As a result of the myriad of rules and regulations, we decided to adopt the KISS (keep it simple, stupid) plan in regards to the class. Rather than carry in loads of books and assigned reading or having to clear CD or DVD discs, we opted to keep the class simple and insular with very few guest speakers. The in-class writing and the ReadBacks, interrupted by the odd lesson or two, became the central elements of our curriculum. This was yard time, hard time, their time, a principle to which we strictly adhered.

By far the most troubling aspect of our H-Unit prison yard "campus" is the long and expanding "hot meds" line, located right outside the door of our classroom. Over the years, we've seen that line grow to enormous proportions. Some call it "better prison through chemistry"—hot meds is an array of psychotropic drugs prescribed and dispensed to inmates holding proper ID. (A sign on the meds window reads: No ID, No Meds.) The dispensing of hot meds each evening can turn the most diligent student Pavlovian. Once the meds window begins dispensing drugs, some students jump out of their chairs to head for the door, rejoining the ranks a few minutes later, medicated under an assortment of mood drugs, be it Ritalin, Wellbutrin for bipolar disorders, and many others including morphine and methadone. One apothecary prescription noticeably absent: medical marijuana, which didn't stop us from smelling the occasional waft of pot smoke lingering out on the yard. When we tried to address this hot meds distraction, we had to recognize that we were dealing with a medical issue, and that we couldn't deprive a student of their prescribed meds.

Like everyone else, we heard the stories and whispers about the black market drug scene. Like when a pill dispensed to a black man is knowingly sold to a white man, which results in somebody getting soundly beaten up for a seemingly insignificant racial faux pas. We soon learned that what's seemingly insignificant and meaningless to the outside world can be absurdly magnified on the inside, particularly if it involves race. For outsiders like us, the prison yard became a learn-as-you-go commonsense experience. We learned that, when in doubt, don't say it, or better yet, don't do it, and especially don't purposely or inadvertently bring prescription drugs, legal smokes, or cell phones on your person.

The reality remains that many an inmate uses prescribed psychotropic drugs to get them through the depression and loneliness of incarceration, which is not without its sense of irony. One evening while waiting outside for our class to be announced and for the classroom door to be unlocked, a medicated inmate who had just left the hot meds line, a homeless-looking hippie Deadhead type, turned to us, scratching his head.

"I don't get it. They put me in here for taking drugs, and then they give me drugs."

Prison is definitely a complex psychological experience, and occasionally we'd attract students known as J-Cats, named after Category J in the California Penal Code, referring to inmates who are "mentally unstable or require psyche drugs to maintain." Not all J-Cats are created equal, we learned, nor are they exclusively crazy, incoherent, or stupid. Some are extreme creative types who can barely function in society sans heavy meds. A lot of J-Cats are the same homeless street people we tiptoe around on city streets, whose transgressions consist mainly of poverty, loneliness, and unorthodox behavior. In H-Unit, the other inmates tend to tolerate the eccentricities of the J-Cats, while at the same time keeping tabs on them just in case something sets them off, endangering the rest of the room. (Once again, the classroom "bodyguard syndrome" comes into play.)

One night during our first few months of teaching, a tatty inmate named Ajax burst through the door after class, carrying a banged-up guitar (no case) and a cache of colorful sketches. He claimed to be part of the original Haight Ashbury hippie movement, and damned if we didn't vaguely recall hearing about a character named Ajax back in the day as part of Blue Cheer's entourage. Blue Cheer was, of course, one of the early, if not the very first, heavy metal power trios, and their only national hit was a speed-addled version of Eddie Cochran's "Summertime Blues."

Ajax's drawings were the work of a mad genius: hand-colored, photo-quality drawings beautifully reconstructing a panoramic view from atop Mount Tamalpais in Marin County, the same mountain that overlooked our nightly trek back up and down the road to and from the main East Gate. The photographic clarity and vivid detail of his drawings were astounding. After showing us the artwork that he carried in his small cardboard box, he asked us if we wanted to hear a song. Or, better yet, did we have a request?

Keith took a stab in the dark. "How about 'Guitar Town' by Steve Earle?"

Ajax shook his head and chuckled, as if to say, "Steve Earle? Piece of cake." He tuned his guitar, strummed the opening chords and whipped through a frenzied version of "Guitar Town," faithful to Steve Earle's pioneering country punk cadence, only faster and more forceful. After he finished the song, Ajax bowed, collected his guitar and his drawings, and walked back out the door, leaving the both of us slack-jawed and stunned. We didn't see him again until he reappeared on the yard a few months later. Then—poof!—he disappeared again, a phenomenon who flashed across the yard like a flickering, burnt-out shooting star.

While we heard stories of confrontations between inmates and CO's, the vast majority of CO's who dealt with us treated us with respect. Most of the interactions that we witnessed between the inmates and the guards were usually civil, even cordial. Outside of a few grouchy CO's, those lording over the H-Unit yard seemed to run a relatively tight ship. That's not to say that during hot summer days or around holidays, tensions didn't run high at times or that underneath the system didn't lie corruption and violence. Like the time in 2007 when one of the dorms in H-Unit erupted into a full-scale riot, which quickly spread to the neighboring buildings. Gas and non-lethal guns shooting blunt projectiles were dispersed. Classes and programs were suspended for nearly two months while investigations were conducted, which resulted in the shipping out of certain ethnicities who were acting out their differences with the other races.

Unlike at institutions such as Los Angeles County Jail where beatings routinely take place and where even correctional officers are exposed for forming gangs, we never witnessed any of the kind of blatant mistreatment that have precipitated hunger strikes and other forms of inmate protest throughout the California state prison system. That's not to say we didn't have students who found themselves thrown in the Hole or who were bullied and mistreated. The H-Unit gossip mill was regularly abuzz with stories of how certain inmates who missed a couple weeks of classes ended up in "the Hole"—Administrative Segregation ("Ad Seg")—or worse, were shipped out altogether to a more stringent Level 3 or 4 institution.

Many times, even the smartest, most together inmates surprised and disappointed us. Like the devout Mexican Raider fan whose aspiration was to counsel kids against gang behavior, but was later busted for possessing sensitive personal information regarding Yardtime gang affiliations. Or the student who was caught passing around sensitive information on individual inmates guilty of sex crimes who were populating the yard. (Prison yard politics dictate that newly arriving inmates present their papers to shot-callers to make sure they're not sex offenders. Otherwise they're usually assaulted, then shuffled off to PC, protective custody.) We soon learned not to be surprised by anything or anybody, and to assume nothing. Often, while tabulating our attendance sheet, we would have to excuse a student who was serving time in the Hole, usually for fighting or social insubordination. Other times, a star student one week might disappear from H-Unit the next week after "PCing out," due to the threat of violence or possibly mounting drug or gambling debts.

The most dramatic example of a student being in the wrong place at the wrong time and getting sent to the Hole was an inmate writer named Dave, who sat in the back corner of our class by the door, and who wrote an at-large column for the *San Quentin News*. He found himself a victim in the crossfire of a prison identity theft and cell phone smuggling ring. Dave was drawn in by the investigative dragnet and sent directly from his job at the print shop to the Hole—no stopping off at his bunk or locker to pack up. Since inmates are usually presumed guilty until proven innocent, Dave, whose identity had been stolen, spent the first few nights on a bunk and bare mattress without a blanket, clean clothes, a toothbrush, or eating utensils. After almost two weeks inside Ad Seg, and after the investigation verified his status as a victim and not a perpetrator, he reemerged back onto the H-Unit yard noticeably thinner, paler, and understandably pissed off. But rather than stew in his misfortune, Dave put pen to paper and wrote of his experiences in the *San Quentin News*. Barely a word of his published account was censored or edited.

Another casualty of the Ad Seg Hole was Safferstein, our version of Arnold Horshack from *Welcome Back, Kotter's* Sweathogs. Safferstein was a tall, gangly Jewish kid in his late twenties or early thirties (you never know, as prison tends to age a person quite rapidly). Safferstein was quite intelligent, if socially awkward, and withdrawn, if not borderline autistic. What was this guy doing inside a state prison?, we asked ourselves. Safferstein spoke a little like Horshack, with a grating whine to his voice. Yet rather than being an object of ridicule in the classroom, the other inmates praised him for his recall talents, particularly his savant ability to remember sports trivia, naming off stats of the previous twenty years of Super Bowl Championships in rapid succession. But Safferstein was a natural writer, and on the subject of "The Last Time I Saw . . . " he wrote a piece recalling his childhood relationship with his grandfather:

> My world was focused on survival, replete with discord. It had lit the place for the days when gas was 75 cents a gallon or when the dollar bought more than a 1-900 phone call. I had to deal with making a living and placating others' pleasures.
>
> Grandpa just wanted to kick back and remember the past. Like when we drove from Pittsburgh to New Jersey to get home. Or the time my family drove from Louisville, Kentucky by way of Indiana, Ohio, and West Virginia before moving back to New Jersey.
>
> It haunts me. The writer of *The Unbearable Lightness of Being* calls this sort of thing "being on the other side of the border." We wanted to connect, but couldn't. Separated by ages and eras, soon we were permanently separated when he died.
>
> I was there for his funeral. Physically, but not mentally.

The last time *we* saw Safferstein was when he turned in this assignment on June 11, 2004. The last we heard of him, according to the H-Unit gossip mill, was that he was attacked in the kitchen, having to defend himself with a broom stick. For whatever reason, he was subsequently shipped out. We, along with Safferstein's classmates—even the tough guys—lamented his sudden departure. We'd unceremoniously lost our Horshack, a solid writer and a comrade-in-arms.

CHAPTER 9

Panthers, Wardens, and Arsons

In January 2006, our tenth book was published. *Huey: Spirit of the Panther* was our first biography on a subject who was no longer living. Huey P. Newton, the mercurial co-founder and leader of the Black Panther Party, had died in 1989, shot in the head inside a crack house. We worked with David Hilliard, a close associate of Newton's who had served alongside him as the Black Panther Party's Minister of Information. Since Hilliard headed up the Huey P. Newton Foundation, the book was an authorized biography. Newton was a cerebral and complex character who spearheaded the Black Power movement in 1968 and was a tortured but genius political thinker and activist.

Just before *Huey* hit the stores, to inject some vocational relevance into the class at San Quentin, we passed around preliminary copies of the cover artwork to gauge the class's opinion. (It got a thumbs-up.) We circulated bound galleys and early copyedited manuscripts to show our students precisely what authors receive throughout the process before their books hit the stores. The class learned that the most exciting aspects of writing a book end well before it actually hits the store shelves. By then, prolific authors are already gearing up for their next work.

At this point we approached our third anniversary of "Finding Your Voice on the Page" at H-Unit. We had learned two things about incarceration: One, that California had a real problem with criminal recidivism. Sixty-seven percent of jailed criminals would return. Two, once a person entered into the criminal punishment revolving door, the state prison system had a "y'all come back now" attitude towards their return. Recidivism served as a large budget bonanza in which the prison industrial complex flourished, right down to overtime wages for the powerful CO union that held California lawmakers in a tight fiscal headlock. Incarceration, we found out, provided private prison enterprises with lucrative state contracts for providing prescription drugs and meds, long distance phone usage, food, supplies, and other amenities, not to mention billions towards construction of new prison buildings, including a brand spanking new San Quentin death row (yet to be built). We immediately saw that if a "knucklehead" repeat offender was dim-witted enough to get into trouble again and again or violate his parole, he would be gladly bounced right back inside the system, serving more time for repeat violations than for the crime he was originally sentenced for to begin with. Plus, the labyrinthine sentencing structures were overly complicated due to three-strike laws and determinate sentencing regulations meant to keep the civilian population safe. That was why, during our first three years, we would see students gleefully reenroll in the class once they returned to H-Unit. It was odd. While we were secretly pleased to retain a talented writer, we were saddened to see him locked up yet again.

Still, we were fortunate enough to welcome more and more new writers to the class. One was a white guy in his late fifties who had come from Mendocino and who implied in his writing that he'd been jailed on a cocaine-dealing beef. Willie W had an interesting history. As a youth, he'd been a Ford male model in New York and had traveled around the world in various professional capacities. As the months of his imprisonment passed, we watched him grow his beard and gray hair until he looked like a cross between George Washington and Benjamin Franklin. Willie had a wide cultural palette and was well-versed in literature, poetry, and the arts. He'd operated a recording studio in Mendocino prior to being arrested. During our last class in December 2005, we surreptitiously passed out Christmas cards which featured a work by our favorite painter, a canvas done in yuletide red and white graduated hues. Willie not only recognized the work by the abstract expressionist artist Mark Rothko, but he recalled its title, *White Over Red*. (We savored the irony of three dozen tough inmates stuck in the penitentiary with our artful Rothko Xmas cards next to their bunks during the holiday season.) Willie quickly volunteered to be our clerk, processing attendance sheets, registering new students into the class, and circulating the sign-in sheet at the start of each class. He was so enthusiastic and appreciative; each Friday, he'd shake our hands and thank us for taking the time to come in.

According to Willie, the judge had thrown the book at him in court. (But that's what they all say.) A five-year sentence represented his very first stint in prison, and Willie was having trouble doing his time and having to circulate among so many inmates with seemingly half his intelligence. By the time he was transferred to H-Unit and found our class, it became an important lifeline, enabling him to finish his sentence one week at a time, on a Friday-by-Friday basis, looking forward to the next "Finding Your Voice on the Page." At first we thought of him as just another convict apple polisher. But soon we realized how serious he was about his reliance on the class when he wrote eloquently, for an assigned in-class writing topic entitled "My Space," about his arrest and the sudden loss of personal freedom:

> It was only a bit more than a year ago, I gazed off my balcony of My Space overlooking the Noyo River which flowed into the ocean nearby. I could lie in my California king-sized bed. Looking

out between my feet was this beautiful, newly-built bridge inviting the river into the ocean. I could use the opposing cliffs on either side of the bridge as a means of telling what time of year it was, by where the sun would set on the horizon.

Then a knock at the door.

The beautiful maidens are, in a moment, stripped of a lifetime's composure and social graces. In bursts the Task Force. On go the lights. Down go the revelers. Down on their bellies on the carpet. On go the handcuffs. Away go the smiles. Suddenly the sumptuous surroundings are torn asunder. The luxury is in instant upheaval. Panic runs rampant; the intimate coterie is separated and carted away in bondage.

The dust settles months later. Where the once wise witness of the sea had been, in its place the walls of a cell hold me. No more beauties, no more whiskey, no more sacraments. All that's left of a life so sumptuous is the solemn reminiscences of a once spoiled person and the consolation of his fellow conscripts.

Another student who joined the class on two separate occasions, once as a repeat parole violator, was a streetwise hipster scribe named Joseph H. Joseph's prose vividly re-created San Francisco's seedy red-light district, bordered by Larkin Street to the east and Van Ness Avenue to the west, O'Farrell Street to the north and Turk Street to the south. He immortalized the transvestites, hookers, dopers, and hustlers that peppered the area. Joseph was tall and skinny, pale white with sullen eyes and long dark tied-back hair—a young Eddie Bunker, Jack Kerouac, and Charles Bukowski rolled into one. When we assigned a writing exercise entitled "Our Gang/ Your Gang" (using vintage pics of the L'il Rascals), Joseph revisited the fringe-types from his old Tenderloin neighborhood:

Cassie is an old school hooker dressed in calf-high black go-go boots, leather minis, and tube tops. Busty 5'8", most of the other girls in the 'hood hate her. Of course she's a favorite with the homeboys. Picture a buxom blonde in torn fishnets, black vinyl, no panties EVER. Her most memorable line to me would be 'If I'm out, meaning passed out, just climb on!' Gotta love her . . . Homeboy Tommy, Tommy K, is doing dope until cross-eyed and chin-chested as Kelly panhandles in front of McDonald's at Golden Gate 'n' Van Ness. She'll give you head for a hit, but careful, the bitch has crabs. Not just one variety, but several . . . Pops runs the Bodega we sell our stolen shit to. You know, booze, hygiene products, batteries, *cases* of shit, mind you, not singles—never singles. Pops is from Turkey, 20 years, same store on Divisadero. Pops is 50, Turkish, silver hair. Ma's his old lady. Traditional Muslim, chunky, veiled. I love Ma 'n' Pa. They look out for me when chips are down.

For over a year we had a father and son as students. Bobby and Billy came from the Northwest, Washington state. Bobby had sandy red hair, a missing front tooth, and loved to talk about riding his Harley-Davidson through the backwoods roads hugging the Canadian border. He wrote horrifying tales about an abusive father who fed him heavy intravenous drugs and blotter acid as a pre-teen. He soon fell into the throes of methamphetamine and was jailed for false imprisonment when he threw an adversary in the trunk of his car and drove around for hours tweaked out on crystal meth. His nineteen-year-old son, Billy, was a handsome drifter out of Santa Cruz who loved to smoke pot and skateboard until he was convicted of selling large amounts of ganja to a group of undercover cops. Billy was released before Bobby, and we watched Bobby fret when Billy didn't write or reach out to him on the phone while out on parole. Bobby served his time and returned to the rural Northwest. Like many devoted classmates, he earnestly promised to write or e-mail, but never did.

Teaching inside a prison environment only sharpened our abilities to size people up quickly. While it's not difficult to spot troublemakers and recidivists, it's perplexing when a seemingly well-behaved Christian is sitting in the class in CDCR blues, looking like he doesn't belong behind bars. Such was the case for a con we'll call Ross.

While it's not our style to ask inmates about another man's crimes, we couldn't help but wonder about mild-mannered, religious Ross. "What's a nice guy like Ross doing inside a state prison like San Quentin?" we respectfully and discreetly asked his H-Unit bunkie out on the yard after class.

"Interesting you should ask," he said. He told us about Ross and how he and a business partner operated a workshop near Sacramento that customized dune buggies and go-carts. One day Ross came home to find his partner in bed with his wife. Since the philandering couple hadn't heard him enter the house, Ross sneaked back outside, casually grabbed a large can of gasoline from the garage, emptied it on his friend's late model pickup truck and set the vehicle alight.

"What Ross didn't realize," our convict friend explained, "was that in the state of California, if you commit arson, you go straight to prison, even if you have no prior convictions."

Let that be a lesson to would-be arsons.

During our tenure in the H-Unit education classroom, we have seen over a half-dozen wardens come and go. Some were visionaries—Jeanne Woodford and Jill Brown, for instance. As previously mentioned, Woodford was the architect of the Success Program. Jill Brown served as warden during 2004 and 2005. She worked for 35 years as a public servant and 25 of those years in the upper echelons of the CDCR system in the state capital. She has the broadest knowledge of the California prison system of anyone we know, and was a valuable source of advice on any correctional questions we had.

On a couple of occasions we would notice a newly painted warden's name on the East Gate. One such appointee instituted a tough stand on free staff volunteers. One day, upon entering the H-Unit yard, we were searched with metal-detector wands. Canvas bags filled with teaching materials were suddenly banned. We were then told we would only be allowed to bring a bottle of water and that writing materials like pens and legal tablets were to be kept in a locked cabinet and counted at the end of each class session by one of the officers.

Then, to the rescue, came a newly appointed disciplinarian, a former warden named Robert Ayers who had stepped out of retirement for a limited return. Ayers had a background as a hard-as-nails, ex-tactical squad correctional officer. Yet, sporting a shaved head and his trademark wide-brimmed hat, Ayers was an enlightened correctional executive. He realized that education was a valid method of cutting down on recidivism and troublemaking on the yard. He understood that if a yard full of jailbirds got hooked on education, they were far less likely to cause trouble and lose their privileges. Ayers became one of the most progressive wardens we ever saw. Soon our pens and paper were no longer held hostage, locked up, and counted. When he came down to visit H-Unit and was told that only certain inmates confined to certain dorms were eligible to take classes, he asked the very same question that had been nagging us:

"Why can't all H-Unit inmates qualify for educational classes?" asked Warden Ayers. "What difference does it make?"

Excellent question! Suddenly the floodgates were open, and we saw class attendance spike again with more new faces. We noticed an influx of more hardcore felons, guys who had been in the system longer, sometimes decades, who were serving sentences longer than just a few years and had many stories to tell. We gladly rolled with the changes as the writing got darker and edgier.

It all went to show, you never know who's on whose side and who believes in what. Judging from his past reputation, we would have judged and pigeonholed Warden Ayers as a strict law and order guy. Except that he showed incredible insight. From that point on,

the playing field was leveled, as all H-Unit inmates had a shot at joining the Success program and signing up for "Finding Your Voice on
the Page." It opened up a whole new vista for us. We had the whole
yard from which to attract new talent, and we soon stumbled upon a
unique and crazy way to recruit more students into the rustic cinder
block classroom we called home every Friday night.

CHAPTER 10

The Tale of the Teutuls

One of the basic realities of writing books for a living is that when the phone rings, it can be a call that alters the path of your life for months, and sometimes years, to come. That's what happened when we received a call from Scott Waxman, New York agent extraordinaire. Often when a celeb or a public figure scores a book deal, hired guns like us are required to help flesh out or write their stories based on extensive interviews, not unlike director Roman Polanski's *The Ghost Writer* film starring Ewan MacGregor as "the Ghost." The first part of Polanski's movie is fairly accurate, especially in the formative scenes that show the protagonist rolling tape and interviewing his client, in his case the ex-Prime Minister of Great Britain, played by Pierce Brosnan, and then inheriting a sorry manuscript that is in severe need of rewriting.

It's happened to us, being brought in as writers or sometimes as "book doctors" to do massive rewrites on a book that's on the verge of being c-c-c-cancelled—the dreaded C-word—by the publishing powers-that-be. Agents and editors are freaking out. The client is bummed. Deadlines are in danger. Money has to be returned. Commissions go kaput. That's until we come in with our laptops and fire hoses, snatching a doomed project out of the clutches of the C-word and rescuing it for publication.

How fast an editor wants a book finished can depend on a publisher's quarterly projections and annual numbers. Publishing is first and foremost a business. That's why even East Coast liberal-minded editors have little or no compunction about publishing books by people like Sarah Palin or Glenn Beck. It's about the cash, baby, and making those numbers! Liberal media bias, our asses!

It was almost two years that we'd been teaching our SQ class when Waxman called us about working with the kinetic and tempestuous Teutul family, famous for their television series, *American Chopper,* or as their company is officially called, Orange County Choppers. The Teutuls had just signed a book deal and they needed writers like us. We met in upstate New York near the town of Newburgh in the Hudson River area.

Our face-to-face meeting went well. The Teutuls were real people. Their workplace had an energetic and competitive vibe. It was obvious that the friction between Paul Senior and his two sons, Paul Junior and Michael, was real and not manufactured or staged for the television cameras. The OCC shop guys—Vinnie, Rick, Jason, Jim Quinn, Steve Moreau—who we'd watched on TV working, assembling bikes, running the biz, were cool, down-to-earth fellows. After volleying a few questions around the table, we handed out a few of our books, most notably *Hell's Angel* by Sonny Barger and John Lydon's autobiography, *Rotten.* It was suggested that Mikey (Michael) take us on a nickel tour of the OCC plant while the others discussed whether or not to hire us.

Walking around, scoping out the OCC shop, Mikey assured us that the gig was probably ours. As he showed us around the shop, we passed a shelf upon which rested a pile of hand-autographed four-color photographs, picturing all three Teutuls kicking back on three magnificent custom bikes. When we asked for one, Mikey graciously reached over and handed us the entire stack.

When he handed us the revered pile of photos, a lightbulb went off in Kent's head. In teaching our class, we were looking for just the right currency that we could bring inside San Quentin to use as "educational materials" but also to spread good cheer and pass the word about our class to attract more new talent from the H-Unit yard (read: bribe people). Once we got back to Oakland, over the next several Fridays we used every photograph placard that Mikey had given us. A couple of the CO's were avid Harley bike riders. They might appreciate a pic or two. But mainly we held drawings at the end of each class. Whoever got their name pulled out of Kent's Guns N' Roses baseball cap won an autographed picture of the Teutuls on their choppers. The only catch: we waited until the final ten minutes to draw the winner, and you had to be "present to win."

Those photos put us on the map on the San Quentin H-Unit yard. Every weekly drawing served its purpose beautifully, as class attendance grew steadily each and every week. Giving away the final photograph, we asked one of the bikers in the class to step up, front and center, and pull the final name out of the Guns N' Roses cap. Allen N. was a tough kid who had written stark descriptions of being abused by a cruel alcoholic stepdad while trying to protect his mother (and himself) from the occasional brutal beating. When Allen stepped up and (legitimately) pulled his own name out of the cap, we were sure he was going to bust a gasket as he broke into a victorious dance of joy. He was like an ecstatic six-year-old on Christmas day, and it was quite moving to watch this guy, who had probably never won anything in his tough life, emerge from his shell so triumphantly, waving the signed picture in the air. We only wished the Teutuls had been in the room to witness the occasion. They would have dug seeing an imprisoned biker go absolutely bananas over winning an autographed photograph of our three famous bike rider clients resting on their laurels and not on their Harleys.

CHAPTER 11

The Dark Side of the Yard

2006. After handing out the Teutuls' pictures and cultivating a steady buzz on the H-Unit yard, we watched our attendance rise while the quality of the writing (and hopefully the teaching) improved. At first we speculated that we were getting the goodie-two-shoes of the yard, the elite, the smarter upperclassmen, the guys who'd seen the light, who were "done" with prison, and had decided to change for the benefit of their families and their children. All fine and good, except the elite men on the yard weren't exactly the audience we were shooting for. We'd hoped to attract a cross-section of the yard population, not only by race, but by subgroup as well.

Then we caught a couple of breaks. Whenever an influential inmate signed up for our class, whether they were a shot-caller or someone else well-respected on the yard, it benefited us. Enter a buffed-out, dashingly handsome white inmate named Big Bob. Big Bob walked into the class and planted himself in the middle of the back row. He was the "poster child" for the Success Program. He kept himself in great shape and carried himself confidently. He had an equally great rapport with the men on the yard as he did with the CO's. Since the banning of weight piles, Big Bob had kept up a rigid exercise regimen that included burpees, isometrics, and push-ups. You could tell Big Bob had been in the system for a while. When we met him, he had served 80 percent of a four-year sentence for a seemingly minor beef involving a stolen pack of cigarettes at a convenience store. Big Bob's past had been plenty sordid, including burglaries and an accidental homicide conviction having to do with an altercation involving him and a crack dealer.

Big Bob was no dummy. He was like a character straight out of *Cool Hand Luke* or *The Longest Yard,* with a college degree in environmental studies. He ran H-Unit's weekly football pool during the NFL and college football seasons. Until San Quentin had formally banned tobacco, Big Bob ran his outfit by banking a large inventory of tobacco pouches, soups, and assorted treats in lieu of money.

Depression ran far and wide in Bob's family and his father had committed suicide. Depression was the ghost that constantly haunted Big Bob, especially once football season ended. Remnants of Big Bob's past included a tattoo written in script below his Adam's apple that read, "Thank God I'm White." Yet by the time we met, Big Bob had long disavowed himself of any white power movement.

Seated in the back row next to Big Bob was his entourage, which we called "the Bigs." Next to Big Bob sat Big Jon. Big Jon was a jovial, broad-shouldered man with a cherubic and kind face. If H-Unit had its Paul Bunyon or John Henry, he was it. Next to Big Jon was Big Head. Big Head wore short pants all year round. After he quickly assimilated into the class, Big Head sat next to us at our table on Registration Day, collaring new students.

"Hey you! Come over here and sign up for this class. These are the Zimmermen. Trust me, you're gonna love this class."

Obviously it was difficult to say "no" to Big Head, and thanks to his persuasive recruiting techniques, our class attendance grew more.

Sitting next to Big Head was Martucci. Martucci reminded us of an Italian short order cook, the guy who looked at home behind the restaurant fryer—or at the local Italian social club—except that Martucci possessed a different talent. He was the in-demand H-Unit barber, who could work stylish miracles with a set of illicit clippers.

The Bigs had created a strong presence in the classroom. As a writer, Big Bob prevailed with the most natural talent, although Big Jon could write quite explicitly about his street adventures. Nobody could re-create a high speed car chase on paper like Big Jon. Just having the Bigs situated in the back of the room made teaching inside a prison a little less . . . foreboding. Should any trouble go down, we assumed that we could solve our own problems internally, although at one point we did step in and become proactive.

With our white attendance on the ascent, we caught a break when one week Freeman walked into the room and took a seat. Having Freeman sign up for the class immediately boosted our attendance among the black inmates, both among the OG's and the young guys from SoCal and Compton. Slowly we were achieving our goal of having the class closely reflect the actual demographics of the H-Unit yard. Surveying the room, we admired the diversity of race and age. Plus, everybody got along—black, white, brown, and other.

Unfortunately this was not the case with Dexter, a gangly young black student who had ADHD issues. Based on his age, we surmised that Dexter might have begun life as your proverbial short-attention-span crack baby. Dexter had a difficult time staying seated for the duration of the entire class. He would often pop up, walk over to the door, and gaze out the window, watching the activity out on the yard. While Dexter was a mild distraction, speculating on his condition, we let him slide, which turned out to be a mistake on our part.

Some of the white students became increasingly annoyed with Dexter's restlessness, so much so that his behavior was interpreted as a show of disrespect to us as teachers and as volunteers. After one class, we were approached by a delegation of students who had tired of Dexter's distractions. If Dexter wasn't willing to show respect, then they would take matters elsewhere—that is, sit down with the black shot-caller on the yard, and possibly have Dexter disciplined by his own kind. It put a whole new spin on the concept of classroom discipline. We didn't need to be hit on the head with a shovel to realize what that might entail. What we didn't want was for Dexter to be "reprimanded" because of our inability to keep order.

We told the white students to hold off, and that it was our fault and we needed to tighten the reigns not only on Dexter, but on anybody else whose behavior interfered with the flow of the class. That night, on the way home, we wondered how many public or private schoolteachers dealt with a discipline issue like possibly crossing a shot-caller.

After a couple of weeks, and a word with Dexter, he disappeared, released or transferred—an example of the constant churn we were experiencing as students came and went. But we got used to the churn, a constant parade of new and interesting faces that walked through the classroom door. Still, we often wondered: who determines where a certain inmate goes, and why?

Which prison an inmate is sent to is part of a methodology that carefully assesses and balances security requirements with individual inmate needs. It turns out that dispersing prisoners throughout any state or federal system is an inexact science, but it's still an art. Newly admitted inmates are constantly run through a litany of evaluations, including medical and mental health screenings. Lots of information is then compiled to develop individual profiles of each inmate. An offender's crime, social background, education, job skills, health history, prescription needs, and criminal record (including prior prison sentences) are all elements that go into the decision of who goes where and why. Background information and the severity of their crimes are then calculated into a point structure that dictates what institution level an inmate is assigned to, with Level 4 being the most severe and secure, and Level 1 being the least supervised. Based on accumulated data, inmates are then matched with the most appropriate custody classification and prison.

San Quentin's actual level rating is difficult to pin down. It ranges from H-Unit, a Level 1 and 2 comprised of dorms with "secured perimeter fences and armed coverage," to the more secured lifers' area up on North Block, and then all the way up to Condemned—or Death Row—hitting the top scale of a Level 4. Even Death Row has its variable levels, the most intense being the "Adjustment Center," the place on the upper yard with foreboding Gothic lettering painted over the doorway entrance. The Adjustment Center is home to the worst of the worst inmates, housing mostly condemned inmates totally incapable of peacefully cohabitating with other human beings. We've heard from even the most seasoned correctional officers that they can feel the evil of the Adjustment Center the moment they walk through the door.

Besides calculating an inmate's points with a prison's level of intensity, other factors contribute to who goes where. Oftentimes an inmate is assigned to a facility that's closer and more convenient for family visits. Most of H-Unit's population was dictated by those shipped in from nearby Northern California counties such as Sac (or Sacramento), Alameda County, Sonoma, CoCo (slang for Contra Costa county) Lake (known for having an abundance of meth cookers and users), and Humboldt (while the latter is known for its meth trade, it's primarily [in]famous for its most famous cash crop, top-quality marijuana).

As a result, we've had several inmates skilled in the growing, sale, and marketing of "alternative horticulture." One notable example was Shawn, a white, dreadlocked, off-the-grid rural communalist who had done time as a youngster in Georgia's penal system. Shawn was arrested in Northern California, or so he claimed, for possession of a quantity of mushrooms. After his conviction, Shawn refused to sign up for drug treatment, claiming that he neither had a drug problem nor was he an addict. So in lieu of drug treatment, Shawn, another prolific writer, served about 14 months, ending up on the H-Unit yard and starring in the short-lived A&E reality series, *San Quentin Film School.*

One of the dangers of frequenting a prison environment is becoming too fascinated by the internal racial politics, something that never interested us. That's not to say that we were naïve to the harsh realities. We fully understood that when the shit is about to fly and inmates are "suited and booted" for war, they are forced to fight alongside their own kind. As teachers, it was necessary to take a neutral position on racial matters. Just nod your head and don't try to admonish or defend anything.

The state keeps tabs on its inmates by sorting them by race, a concept that seems odd and outdated—and in the civilian world, illegal. As a result, strange prison alliances occur between racial factions. For example, Northern Mexicans, *Norteños,* may side with black inmates against *Sureños,* their Southern brethren. While the majority of Americans strive for an equal opportunity, color-blind society, the prison yards maintain an outmoded climate of racial and regional segregation. The categories start out general: Whites, Blacks, Mexicans, and Others. Then groups are subdivided again— for example, Mexicans into *Norteños* and *Sureños*—and are even further broken down into subgroups like the "paisa," a semi-derogatory term for rural northern Mexicans. Out on the H-Unit yard, certain tables or portions of the yard, even pay phones, are claimed or designated by race. It's the old adage: divide and conquer, because it's far easier to control smaller, disunited camps than a large united front.

Even more specific are the "cars." A car is a prison subgroup that sorts inmates further by lifestyle—bikers, transsexuals, gays, whatever—or by geography. A car might bear the name of a city, county, or even an area code. Such is life in an environment where inmates are willingly branded and categorized. Conversely, as teachers, it became our mission to teach and to appeal to everybody on a neutral, nonracial basis. A classroom's status as a "demilitarized" sanctuary enabled us to run our program without having to bow to the racial demands of the prison yard.

There was one time the race issue worked harmoniously when one of our white students, Ray C, asked us if he could list us as a sponsor for an event he was trying to put together out on the H-Unit yard.

Ray was an industrious sort. A simple room designated as the nondenominational chapel doubled as a music room where inmates could hold impromptu jam sessions at night, grinding out heavy metal and funk. Ray carried his electric bass guitar in a gig bag almost everywhere he went. As an incarcerated musician, he missed jamming with his friends, so Ray set out to organize a music festival right out on the H-Unit yard! Once we found out, we gladly yielded our usual Friday evening time slot and became the sponsors of Ray's festival.

Come the day of the "fest," Ray and another inmate dragged a small Peavy PA system out onto the yard. Then came the instruments, guitar amps, speaker cabinets, and a drum kit that was stashed in the closet of the chapel. With barely enough extension cord to extend his stage out onto the dirt, Ray had erected a makeshift bandstand to present a three-bill concert.

The opening act was a group of Mexicans, comprised of both Southern and Northern musicians playing the music of their homelands. The music sadly yearned for freedom and family. As the loosely rehearsed musicians struggled through a thirty-minute set, more and more inmates gathered in front of Ray's makeshift festival.

During the show, we cruised the yard looking for a table to sit at. Turned out they were already claimed, so we opted to join the standing crowd. The second band was comprised of black inmates and featured a tight set of funk and soul music, including punchy James Brown covers mixed in with some crooning soul ballads. As the blacks' set progressed, the musicians shifted from song to song, giving a variety of inmates the opportunity to sit in. Turns out, the depth of talent that populated the H-Unit yard was promising. Chicken-scratching guitarists. Grooving drummers. Popping bassists. The blacks had assembled one hell of a band, as tight and funky as the Latinos were mournful and sad. After a forty-five minute set, it was time to make way for the headliner.

Ray used his status as festival organizer to close out the show, and close the show he did. With a set of predominantly white rock musicians, Ray's band broke into a faithful version of Pink Floyd's "Dark Side of the Moon." It was clear that Ray had rehearsed his band long and hard, as the intricacies of Roger Waters' and David Gilmour's music were presented almost verbatim, note for note. As we scanned the yard, we saw skinheads next to blacks, next to Mexicans, all digging Ray's Pink Floyd tribute band. There we stood, together, as Ray's festival progressed peacefully and incident-free.

It was a rarefied San Quentin moment. We saw the gun towers and the razor wire surrounding the perimeter, the ducks quacking around the yard, the volleyball court with no net, the Native American sweat lodge, and the empty chow hall. We stood among the inmates, huddled around the makeshift stage listening to Ray's encore from *The Wall*, "Comfortably Numb."

We asked ourselves, how could Pink Floyd's music have possibly sounded any better?

It was like a dream, surreal in the moment. San Quentin had assumed its alter-ego identity: from terrible prison to unforgettable music venue, a little like Johnny Cash had experienced many years prior. At that point in time, there was no place on earth we would have rather been than grooving to the sound of Ray's band breathing convict life into Pink Floyd's "Breathe."

CHAPTER 12

Welcome Back

Every Friday night became reminiscent of the 1970's TV sitcom *Welcome Back, Kotter* starring John Travolta, which featured the Sweathogs, an incorrigible but loveable band of classroom losers. We had a consistent stable of guys who could express themselves proficiently on paper. While they couldn't exactly spit out fifty-cent words from the dictionary, they could spontaneously and efficiently put stories, descriptions, thoughts, narratives, opinions, feelings, monologues, rants, remembrances, and recollections straight onto the page in short thirty-minute in-class bursts, a process that's way tougher than it seems. Since bringing cameras inside is a no-no, here's a series of random portraits of a few of the guys that we recall, The Class circa 2007:

Ace was a forty-something tattooed car mechanic and Harley lover, whose tied-back hair made him look as much like a veteran Dead roadie as an inmate. He admired motorcycles, loyalty, and his wife, who patiently awaited his release. "I'll walk with those of whom I am proud, or I will walk alone," he once declared.

Donnie the Kid was a small-time burglar from Bakersfield who, after breaking into an occupied house, got rolled up on a felony beef. He looked barely eligible to vote, much less hold an active CDCR ID number. Donnie was a smart kid who regularly participated in class. Any parent would have been proud to have such an intelligent son, if only he hadn't turned into a bumbling amateur burglar knucklehead.

> I am 21, white, and in prison for burglary. They gave me four years, eight months. Now if you think county jail is hell, just wait until you catch some real time here. I've been down since '05. Doing time is not cool. I can't wait to get back to my life. So if you like to be stressed out, depressed, and all you've got is time, time to worry, time to stress, time to hate life and yourself, then prison is your ticket.

Laughing Wolf was a young, handsome, and slim Native American with long, straight brown hair. Laughing Wolf loved golden oldies and excelled in rock trivia. He was in high spirits when we brought him Top 100 lists from years past pulled off the Internet. Laughing Wolf was a good example of someone in jail not wasting away. Here's his unique take on his typical SQ Fridays and Saturdays:

> Most "outsiders" seem to think that every day of the week is the same for us just because we're doing time. I suppose that may be true if you don't have a good program going, but the reality of it is that most of us do have jobs or go to school! I work four days a week as a teacher's assistant in education Monday through Thursday, and have my classes on Friday. So just like everyone else who works Monday through Friday, I look forward to the weekend. I actually get to sleep in a little bit on Friday morning because my first class, Meditation in Motion, doesn't start until 11:00am. Then after that, I'll go play some handball for a while. But what I really look forward to is having a nice, big late lunch with my good friends Tim and Randy. And it's not your regular bagged lunch we eat. We'll throw in some soups, rice, meat log, scrambled eggs, cheese, whole garlic, etc. . . . and

make burritos. But sometimes it's not about the food, even if all you have is a bagged lunch. What's good about it is that you're spending quality time with your best friends. One thing I miss on Fridays, though, is going to the [Indian] sweat lodge because I have "creative writing" at the same time, so I don't get to spend that quality/spiritual time with my peeps. But I do make up for it the next morning by going to the lower yard to sweat with the lifers. It's a spiritual high for me, and I learn a lot from those guys.

Jordan W, like Ace, was a biker's biker. Like a lot of bikers on ice, he missed the open road, worshipped the Hell's Angels, and carried a snapshot of his rigid frame bike.

Another peckerwood (slang for white inmate), Franklin H, was convicted on a manslaughter beef after beating someone to the Promised Land in a bar brawl. Frank often wrote about toiling in various blue-collar factories and junkyards in Oklahoma. His narratives were filled with close calls and car crashes. We lost him after he gained the confidence to take more classes and earn his GED high school equivalency diploma by taking classes up on the Hill.

Class clown Eric G, a cheeky ex-junkie with reddish blond hair, wore a permanent illegal smirk and a two-day growth on his mug. He was confident and smug until the day came to say adieu before his release. By then, his careless smile had morphed into nerves and fear as we exchanged hugless goodbyes and friendly back slaps. Here's a sample of his writing:

> Being in SQ really does it to me. I can't watch the Sci-Fi Channel. The damned TV is f**ked up and turned up too loud. No porn is allowed. My medication isn't working. The shower is on the other side of the TV, so you've got to shower on display. The five shitters are so close together you bump knees with the guy next to you. Then when I dream of sheep, they don't kiss me back and the little piglets squeal on me. Everything is me, me, me.

Freddie. He was the Cal Ripken, Jr. of the class. Half-druggie, part Mexican, part Native American. He holds the record for attending the most classes, a streak that extended beyond five years. His writing centered on greaser culture, recounting his working-class 1960s youth in Northern California, before rural orchards exploded into booming suburban subdivisions. A typical trip back to the sixties:

> My first car was a '57 Chevy which I got from some poor guy shipping off to Vietnam. This car was a jewel as far as first cars go—a real girl catcher. My first daughter was conceived in the backseat when Petula the Tramp was banged back there on a regular basis. The part I hated was going up to her house and talking to her mom, in essence, asking for permission to bone her daughter on a night out. The drive-in movie lasted longer than two hours, just long enough to take her up to Clyde Hills. You know, she never did say much when she climbed into my pink and gray stock painted '57. Just a small crazy laugh when I asked her for some pussy.

Randy T was brash, belligerent, and confrontational. A two-fisted hard-ass, it was only a matter of time before this guy would run off the rails and test our whistles with an altercation. He would volley smartass comments across the room and taunt the other class members., yet he wrote authoritative and florid prose. Randy was an antisocial bad seed and openly gay but hardly the effeminate type. Randy was a tough nut, looking for trouble, and he would soon find it.

One night just after class we heard the sound of crashing chairs. Franklin lunged at Randy T, flailing wildly, swatting him across the side of his head with a quick flurry of punches and slaps. Keith moved to the front door to block the window while four alert inmates rushed in to separate the two. We had never seen a fight broken up so fast and quietly—it went down in a matter of seconds! Randy T was quickly hustled out the front door, and Kent approached Franklin to calm him down. Nobody from the Watch Office next door heard a peep since we hadn't blown our whistles. We were relieved next week to find that Randy T and his boyfriend were no-shows and had dropped out of the class. The guy had a huge chip on his shoulder. Nobody brought up the incident, and we pretended like nothing happened.

Part of what another student—writing as his alter ego Dinero D the Dynamic "P"—got out of the class was composing the most outlandishly ghetto-ized stories and character lines, and then listening to two twin, middle-aged, white, flat-assed authors read his stuff back to the class. Dinero's prose remains some of our favorite prose to come out of SQ. His were the musings of a black twenty-something pimp from Sacramento's Arden Way. Colloquial. Side-splitting. Misogynist. You could almost hear the howls of laughter and derision from the kindred spirits across the yard. Dinero's writing was intensely vivid and streetwise. Over the past year, he'd spawned a posse of classroom imitators who wrote in the same "urban" hip-hop-bitches-and-hoes jargon and meter. While Dinero's writings were heavily laced with implacable humor, underneath the stylish prose was a cautionary tale of defeat and self-deprecation. In the end, our hero, Dinero D, the Superfly hustler with his cache of flashy "hoes," was consistently left in the dust of betrayal and failure. Whenever it was the street vs. Dinero D, the street always emerged victoriously.

Dinero's style of bravado pimp prose persisted until Halloween 2010, when the in-class writing subject up on the whiteboard was "What Truly Scares Me to Death." It was then that Dinero dramatically dropped his guard for all of us to see.

> I'd be bullshitting myself if I said nothing scares me. Like "real men" ain't scared of nothing. Now, I could write what this whole

class expects me to write: About how I'm scared to death of being hoe-less, broke, and homeless. Sorry, not today. What scares me to death is some serious shit! I'm scared of getting my third strike and spending the rest of my natural life on the shelf with a bunch of self-proclaimed ballers, players, gangsters, and geniuses. Spending my life in a cell surviving on Top Ramen, meat logs, dehydrated refried beans, BBQ chips, and cheese squeeze. Or watching a crummy 13-inch TV. No HBO, no internet, and no pussy. I can't go out like that. No way, not The Kid. I can't be one of the masses standing out there in that meds line trying to escape my pitiful existence.

I've been playing Russian roulette with my life committing crimes, and then praying I don't get struck out. Last time my bail was $1,000,000, and I'm telling the truth, I was scared to f**king death. I thought they was gonna hang my pimpin' ass out to dry. Well, they won't get another chance at me. It's over for me, cuz there ain't no place in "the game" for a muthaf**ka who's scared to death. I'll just write books about the game, and when my first book is published—and I get that first phat-ass check—and when I get my first chance to do a book signing, I'm gonna sign my full name, "Dinero D the Dynamic "P." PS: I'm Rich, Bitch!" on EVERY book.

After reading back Dinero's piece, the class, shocked by his uncharacteristic show of humility, burst into applause.

We decided to break a personal rule and reach out to Steve Ramone after he was released on parole to the working-class bedroom community of Fairfield, California. This was where Steve had first been arrested and convicted, though at the time he'd been living in San Francisco. Ramone and a friend were cruising through town on their way back from Sacramento looking for trouble and they found it in the back of a remote industrial park. A man in a suit was enjoying a nooner with his secretary in the back of his Lexus when Ramone grabbed a table-leg-turned-weapon and forced the discon-certed couple out of the car, attempting to rob and blackmail the man. This being a stupid but violent assault, Steve was apprehended quickly. How hard was it to locate a 350-pound, round-faced white kid on the run with a mass of tattoos, wandering aimlessly around the town? Steve was a serial parole jumper. Before we met him, he'd jumped parole and moved to Greenwich Village where, after 9/11, his file crossed the desk of a parole agent who was prompted to issue a warrant for his arrest. Steve was making pancakes for his girlfriend and her child when he answered a knock at the door, only to find the cops on the other side, guns drawn.

After his next release, we took him to a *Hell's Angel* book sign-ing party at the local Harley dealership near the Oakland Airport. He was so large, he weighed down the passenger side of Keith's Mazda Miata. Stuck in Fairfield on parole, Ramone lived on the streets where he alternated between a pair of homeless shelters while barely scraping by working a day shift at a telemarketing gig. (Ramone vowed to one day write a book on the "art" of living on the streets—where to shower and shave, where to crash, eat for free, stash your stuff, and lay your head without paying rent—while remaining fairly invisible.) It wasn't long before Steve grew restless of the suburbs and disappeared again for the City by the Bay, and apparently jumped parole again.

We last ran into Ramone inside the San Francisco Public Library while researching a book we were writing on the 50th anniversary of the Monterey Jazz Festival. There he was: a larger-than-life tattooed hulk. Careful not to spook him, we approached him from behind and tapped him on the shoulder.

"That you, Ramone?"

Steve turned around briskly and then grinned when he saw we weren't law enforcement agents. We exchanged hushed pleasantries and found an abandoned study area where we could chat briefly.

"I'm livin' in a squat South of Market."

"You okay for cash?"

Ramone shrugged.

We emptied our pockets. Minus what we needed for parking, Kent had twenty-two bucks, Keith fifteen. We handed Ramone thirty-seven dollars.

"Stay cool, Steve."

Weeks later, Kent received a cryptic e-mail sent from an anonymous Internet café. True to form, restless Ramone had bolted San Francisco for Santa Monica. He started up his own MySpace page, and had drawn over 100 new "friends." On the lam and living on the beach with nine months of time still on the state's books, Ramone's cover was blown when he boldly registered for literature and writing classes at a junior college in Santa Monica. After being summoned to the registration office, Steve was apprehended by state authorities. Ramone then suffered through six harrowing months inside the heinous underbelly of the Los Angeles County Jail mini-metropolis, surviving and coexisting alongside the Crips and Bloods. As punishment for fleeing parole yet again, the judge ordered Ramone to serve out the rest of his term in Centinela State Prison, a hot box located on the arid Cali-Mexican border near San Diego, where he broiled in the heat alongside the coyotes and the scorpions. Last we heard he no longer owed the state time until one of our students reported a possible Ramone sighting inside San Quentin's West Block reception area. We hoped Ramone made it back to his native abode in Brooklyn before getting pinched again.

It was a Wednesday when we got a call from the programming head of the Success Program. Oh no. What had we done now? We called her Sinead, after Sinead O'Connor. San Quentin Sinead got her nickname from wearing her hair in a buzz cut similar to the one sported by the real Sinead. We liked working with her. During her time in H-Unit managing the education programs, she was a valuable conduit between volunteers and custody.

SQ Sinead phoned us to ask about possibly cosponsoring an ice cream social to be held inside the H-Unit chow hall.

An ice cream social?

In prison?

Big Bob had recommended she call us. In addition to cosponsoring the event for a couple of hundred bucks, SQ Sinead had another question: Would we have a line on some possible live entertainment—a singer or a comedian?

A couple of C-notes to sponsor an ice cream social wasn't a problem. It was similar to a fantasy we had, to one day drive up to a Wendy's or an In-N-Out Burger joint, order fifty double cheeseburgers and fries, twenty chocolate milk shakes, and twenty Diet Cokes, then sit around the H-Unit Education Classroom with the guys, writing, shooting the bull, eating burgers, and reading stuff aloud.

Come to find out, most major fast-food places *will* bring a cooker inside a prison and prepare their branded food off-site for the inmates. Imagine prison as a fast-food profit line item! We did the arithmetic once, and calculated that if we bought *everybody* on the yard a hamburger, fries, and a shake, it would set us back three or four thousand bucks. One day, we vowed . . .

Thus, two hundred bucks for an ice cream social sponsorship was a bargain. As for entertainment, after putting the phone down, an e-mail beeped into our inbox from folk singer Dan Bern, someone we'd met during our previous lives in the music biz. Dan Bern wrote biting, satirical songs reminiscent of *Another Side of Bob Dylan*.

Dan was a quality songwriter. After leaving his major label deal he'd gone indie and toured the world relentlessly. And it just so happened that he was to be in town on the day of the San Quentin ice cream social. We bounced him back a message.

"How would you like to play inside the walls of San Quentin?"

Bern's reply was instantaneous. "You mean like Johnny Cash? Hell, yeah."

We called back SQ Sinead with not one, but *two* bits of good news for the men. First, we'd gladly kick in a couple of Benjamins towards the ice cream social. Second, we would also gladly supply the entertainment. A few days later everything was confirmed. We put the check in the mail, and Dan was in.

A few days later, a call came in from Sinead.

"This guy Dan Bern, have you heard his song, 'Tiger Woods'?"

"Yeah, what about it?"

"Tiger Woods' balls? He's singing about Tiger Woods' balls! I'm not sure that's going to go down well with the warden."

Tiger Woods' balls? Years before Tiger Woods was busted by his wife Elin for being a shameless ho'chaser and porn star potentate, Dan Bern had written an anthem to Tiger Woods' fabled lower anatomy. At the time the song was written, Tiger reigned supreme in sports for having the largest of *cajones* in winning numerous PGA tournament cups. So yes, we told SQ Sinead, Tiger Woods *does* have big balls, both literally and figuratively. So what?

Our case fell on deaf ears. Dan was outski.

We grudgingly assured Sinead that we would *disinvite* him. Sorry, Dan. Something's come up. Another time? (For the record, let it be known that Tiger Woods' balls cost Dan Bern his San Quentin debut.)

If an ice cream social seems kinda corny, particularly inside San Quentin State Prison, trust us, *it's not.* As we waited outside amid a tight throng of inmates for the chow hall doors to open, a strong aroma of burning primo Northern California weed (likely Humboldt County) wafted among us. A few of the men laughed at the shocked expression on our faces. Weed was the last thing we expected to smell on the H-Unit yard. Still, an ice cream social seemed like the perfect place to develop a case of the munchies.

Inside the mess hall, the warden showed up to address the men and volunteers. The ice cream social was being staged as an incentive to recruit more H-Unit inmates to join the Success education program and to sign up for classes. So the dining hall was full, with lots of smiling faces at every table. The atmosphere was self-segregated but congenial. The blacks stuck to one side of the room while pockets of whites, Mexicans, and "others" were sprinkled throughout the chow hall. A makeshift PA had been set up, playing an inmate's soothing collection of Kenny G-styled smooth jazz. A huge banner had been painted and was plastered on the concrete wall. It read, "San Quentin Inmates Wish to Thank the Zimmerman Brothers." We worked all areas of the room to greet everybody, shaking hands and hanging out with the blacks, whites, browns, etc.

We were just the proud sponsors, and we dug the vibe. Everyone was having a ball socializing and hanging out at the ice cream social. Like Eric Burdon once sang, "Even the cops grooved with 'em." And they did.

Despite the excellent vibes, the Dan Bern-less entertainment left a lot to be desired. Instead of our cutting edge "Alt Folkie" singing about Tiger Woods' balls, a lesbian comedian performed feminist skits. From the looks on the men's faces, it wasn't exactly the female entertainment they'd envisioned. The butch comedian was clad in a loose-fitting Hawaiian shirt, a dead ringer for Greg Allman circa 1975, right down to the long, straight, sandy-colored hair and hormonally-grown goatee soul patch. We longed for Dan's insane, tongue-in-cheek ballads paying tribute to Kurt Cobain and alien abductions . . . or the witty song he wrote about what might have been if Marilyn Monroe had married *Henry* Miller instead of *Arthur* Miller.

It was the best $200 tax write-off we ever spent. The back half of the dining hall was set up with individual food stations. The food was comprised of CostCo bulk products, which met with the CDCR bureaucratic approval. The dessert lines moved quickly and efficiently as inmates wearing plastic gloves and hairnets dispensed gallons of ice cream, baskets of fresh strawberries, piles of cookies, milk chocolate chunks, and slices of carrot and German chocolate cake, served alongside cranberry and orange juice, lemonade, iced tea, and gallons of apple cider. It was an all-you-can-eat affair, as inmates stuffed their faces and their pockets and filled up paper-plates-to-go to take back to their non-student bunkies. No food was wasted.

The SQ ice cream social wasn't without its potential incident. Prior to breaking out the goodies, one well-meaning young volunteer began placing gallon jugs of apple cider at every table. It didn't take long for one of the experienced organizers to react to the faux pas. Every gallon was retrieved, save for one missing jug.

Suddenly the celebratory music stopped.

"Okay," the CO sergeant in charge announced from the front of the hall, "until the last missing gallon of cider is accounted for, we will have to cancel this event."

Most everybody in the room knew perfectly well what would become of the stolen apple cider. It would be smuggled out, stashed somewhere and fermented into "pruno," an illicit and powerful prison booze brewed from the sugars of accumulated fruit. Whoever had bagged the lost gallon of cider was under pressure to cough it up, or else risk the wrath of a roomful of angry cons deprived of their cake and ice cream. Within minutes, the missing jug mysteriously reappeared and the celebration resumed without a hitch.

We walked back to our car that night on two massive highs. One came from the sugar: the ice cream, cookies, and cake we had stuffed our faces with. The other was from the rare opportunity to sponsor, of all things, an ice cream freaking social at San Quentin state pen!

CHAPTER 13

The Magical Box

As another raucous Friday night with the Sweathogs passed, it was sometimes difficult gauging the effects of the class on the home front. While we would come home on a creative high, we missed a lot of quality time with our spouses. As it was, Kent kept radically different hours as a writer than did his wife, who worked equally unconventional hours, dragging herself off to work each morning at 5:30 am, just a few hours after Kent retired. It wasn't quite a "ships passing in the night" day shift/night shift arrangement many working families go through, but close, which made habitually missing every Friday night cause for concern. Trouble was, Kent's wife, Deborah, wouldn't admit to the slight. She was supportive, but it was up to Kent to make sure things didn't get shaky at headquarters.

Wish we could remember the exact spark of the argument that started between Kent and Deborah one Friday night, but like most marital rows, it started out petty and stupid. Kent forgot that he had committed to his wife to accompany her to a semi-important get-together with friends. Trouble was, this was also one of the rare Friday nights when Kent had agreed to cover the class for Keith who had, months prior, committed to take his wife Gladys out to an

Arctic Monkeys concert at the Fox Theatre, Oakland's downtown refurbished concert palace. Ordinarily, there would have been no problem, but Kent had carelessly double-booked himself.

"I thought charity begins at home," Deborah lamented.

Words were said and immediately regretted. Besides, you know you're on shaky ground to begin with when you choose a roomful of criminals over a loyal wife and your brother's Arctic Monkeys concert. Who could blame her for feeling slighted?

That Friday night, it must have shown on Kent's face that things were temporarily strained on the home front. But as advised at our brown card training session, we always tried to maintain a professional distance by not revealing too much of our personal lives. As the authors of 16 books, and with potentially intrusive information about us all over the Internet, it's difficult to stay invisible. Still, we maintained our philosophy that the class was not about us or our writing, unless we were discussing a work in progress that had vocational relevance to the class. In recounting stories about our writing experiences, we were careful not to come across as braggarts or name-droppers. Some of the students were naturally curious about our personal lives and how we maintained social order in the midst of writing and teaching.

Are you guys married?

"Yup."

Kids?

"Nope."

You guys live close to each other?

"Yeah. Nine minutes apart, up in the Oakland hills."

And that was pretty much the extent of us spilling our guts, macho men keeping things from other macho men, until Big Jon raised his hand.

"So, what do your wives think about you guys coming to prison every Friday? Don't they miss having you guys around for the whole weekend?"

Teaching the class solo, Kent tried dodging the question, but did a poor job of covering himself. He looked down and shook his head. "Funny you should ask . . . " his voice trailed off.

It was the kind of thing that can set off a tidal wave of curiosity across the room, especially among incarcerated dudes.

"Look, it's no big deal," Kent said.

Big Jon persisted, "No, what happened?"

"Look, I ran into a little buzz saw on the home front. Let's move on."

The next week just before the class broke up, Big Jon approached the two of us.

"Listen," he said, "Don't leave right away. I've got something for you guys."

After a few minutes, Big Jon came skulking back from his dorm. "Follow me."

At the time, teachers were allowed to venture into the H-Unit dorms to announce their classes. We followed Big Jon to Dorm Five. Months later, when the dorms were suddenly deemed off limits for teachers to enter, we were actually relieved. The H-Unit dorms were muggy and hot inside. Guys stalked around the rooms shirtless, and naked in the shower. There was a constant roar of conversation, and whenever we entered the dorm area, we'd attract a crowd of our students, which would inevitably piss off the third shift CO on duty. Plus, there was a certain indignity in seeing our students confined to their bunks.

Big Jon lived in the far corner of the dorm, next to the window. At the time, the guys who enrolled in the Success Program were segregated into one barrack, supposedly an "honor dorm" of some sort with minor extra privileges like a bigger TV or hotter coffee. Big Jon's bunk wasn't far from Big Bob's. Technically, they were neighbors. We suspected that Big Jon was a craftsman of sorts. He worked construction in the civilian world. On the inside he often picked up a few extra coffees, tobacco pouches, and soups by repairing Walkman headphones for his homies using a tiny hidden screwdriver he had stashed away, which, if discovered by the CO's, would be construed as possessing a weapon.

Big Jon excitedly presented us with two gorgeous jewelry boxes he had made from scratch. We knew that Jon was a craftsman of sorts, but not as ingenious as was evident from what he gave us. The boxes looked like something from Gump's or Bloomingdales, except they were constructed solely of found objects: newspaper, cardboard, stray cloth, and hinges made of string.

Prison art wasn't exactly new to us. We'd seen guys carve cigarette lighter covers and coffee cup holders constructed of wood with a baked-on outer crust made of coffee grounds, sporting an inset Harley-Davidson logo. One student gave us tiny figurines made of folded origami paper and a stemmed rose made of paper that he'd created during class. Or we'd receive full-color greeting cards with waxed, enameled, embossed artwork on our birthday.

But Big Jon's jewelry boxes took the cake.

They were like mini-log cabins, constructed of many strands of tightly wound sheets of newspaper, beautifully tinted using shoe polish, which explained why his fingers were indelibly stained with what looked to be tobacco. Now we knew it was shoe polish. Suddenly it made sense why Big Jon saved all the cardboard he could scrounge up from our finished writing tablets.

Turned out Big Jon's jewelry boxes were coveted items on the yard. One of the boxes he presented to us was light brown, and the other a beauteous smoky gray. Inside each box were separate compartments for rings and earrings, covered in corduroy-like material. (Where he got that, we had no earthly idea.) In the middle of the box was a drawer for necklaces.

The beauty and precision of the boxes left us speechless.

"These are for your wives for putting up with us, and for being cool enough to let you guys come around here on Fridays."

We were awestruck, and didn't quite know what to say. How the hell were we going to get them past the gate?

We stashed the boxes deep in our bookbags and tried to appear nonchalant as we signed out at the gate. As we quickly flapped open each bag, our hearts were in our mouths and our pulses banged in our ears. As we passed the gate threshold and down to the visitor's parking lot, we were breathless as our blood pressure returned to normal. Turned out we had no problems at the gate.

Kent returned home to find his wife sound asleep on the couch. Rather than wake her, he covered her up, pecked her on the cheek and set Big Jon's gift on the ottoman close by.

The next day Deborah perused her special gift. At the bottom of the lacquered box was a hidden drawer. Pulling out the drawer, written on the bottom was an inscription, "Made in SQSP on [date] by Big J . . . " Folded inside the hidden drawer was a note which read:

"Thanks for letting Kent come out to SQSP. It gets us through the week. Respect, the Class."

Kent had never seen his wife so moved and stunned at the same time. The box lives in its honored place upon their mantle, and from that day on, we didn't argue with our wives about Friday nights anymore.

CHAPTER 14

It Was Christmas in Prison . . .

"It was Christmas in prison, and the food was real good," song-writer John Prine once wrote. "We had turkey and pistols carved out of wood."

Turns out Prine wasn't crooning about H-Unit. The only thing out of the ordinary about Christmas chow at San Quentin was the addition of a slab of mystery meat called "turkey ham" at the chow hall. In 2007, Christmas fell on a Tuesday, but the Friday before was the 21st. We considered taking the week off to enjoy the holidays and save our marriages, maybe a weekend in the Napa Wine Country. So, on December 14th we put it to the men.

"So . . . what do you guys do in here for the holidays? Family visits? Phone calls? Bowl games? Christmas cards?"

Ever been in a roomful of simultaneous hangdog faces?

Super dumb question. Out of our unscientific sample of knuckleheads, none were getting family visits. Perhaps a phone call or a Christmas card? It had been a while since most of the guys had received a friggin' Christmas card. When we found out the guys would be spending their holiday locked down with a skeleton correctional staff, we decided, what the hell, let's stick our necks out again. We'd show up on the 21st. Why not?

A few days before class, we hit the streets in search of the coolest holiday cards on the planet. We found them at a place called Avant Card, a high-end greeting card store in downtown San Francisco. They carried a line of holiday cards designed by New York's Museum of Modern Art. There were six cards to a box at fifteen bucks a pop! We spent a hundred bucks for three dozen cards to hand out to convicts. But these babies were super cool and artsy, three-dimensional pop-ups that would proudly adorn any McMansion fireplace mantel, much less a drab bunk in a penitentiary dorm. We went for the decidedly non-religious, spiritually neutral selection with chilly scenes of winter painted in the abstract, a colorful herd of grazing reindeer, embossed decorated trees, and a souped-up Santa's sleigh.

The cards were meticulously dye-cut, vibrantly colored, and had three-dimensionally functional moving parts. Warren Buffett wouldn't have bought such extravagant cards. But we figured, what the hell? Bio Bros. LLC, our little company, had had a decent year in the book writing biz. If these holiday cards brought a scintilla of Yuletide cheer in the absence of a phone call from home or a Christmas dinner, then our mission would be accomplished and we would have taken care of our guys.

Come December 21st, a crisp cold wind blew across the H-Unit yard, which was a blessing in disguise, since a sunlit California Christmas can be as depressing as, well, being stuck in a state penitentiary on Jesus's birthday. The yard was empty and bleak. Not a creature was stirring, not even a mouse or the inmate trash collectors or an armed CO walking the beat.

But we came bearing especially good cheer because sandwiched between our educational materials were our six boxes of posh designer Christmas cards. When the CO's announced the class over the loudspeakers, the men came from all directions, clutching their notebooks and tablets, tottering—never running—towards the classroom door like a flock of powder blue-shirted zombies. We drew an early full house.

"Okay . . . listen up!" Keith announced. "We've got a Christmas surprise for you knuckleheads." The men's eyes widened as we spread out an array of cards across the front table. "Everybody gets just one. No double-dipping, please. There's plenty to go around."

When was the last time you saw anybody absolutely flip out over a Christmas card? The guys sprung out of their chairs and formed a fast line that snaked around the classroom. In minutes, every card was snapped up, as well as the cardboard boxes and clear plastic lids that held them. We boldly signed our names on each card. Only one student, a black Muslim, politely declined our holiday card. We later learned that some inmates passed their cards on to their children, wives, and girlfriends. Had we known, we wouldn't have signed them.

On top of the holiday cards, we really came prepared that night. The previous week's writing assignment was typed up and ready for ReadBack: the Z'men holiday Creative Writing extravaganza, My SQ Christmas! We passed out the holiday edition of *Hard Time, Yard Time, Our Time*. It was time for us to read aloud. Some of the holiday writing was markedly warmer than the usual fare, while some was quite grim and sad.

If our Christmas plan was to try and penetrate the hard protective shells of our student writers using shameless sentimentality, it worked! We were breaking through those tough exteriors. Most of the men recalled vivid childhood memories of past Decembers spent with children, wives, and family. Others lamented somber tales of drunk or abusive parents. We found the writing, both in mood and content, to be delightfully all over the place. Plus, their reminiscences took us across the country.

Shawn, the dreadlocked white boy, wrote a Christmas tale about jumping probation in Wisconsin, ending up in a Nashville Waffle House on his way to Florida, getting picked up by two lasses, and spending the holidays working for their dad. "The dude paid me and gave me a sack of the greenest weed east of Colorado, which, by the way, he grew himself downstairs."

Gerry recalled lording over a 15-bedroom old folks' home dressed as Santa and "our adopted grandparents awoke on Christmas to the smell of holiday food and a big tree with presents under it."

Franklin wryly rhymed, "What the San Quentin menu calls turkey ham, is like calling fresh dog shit strawberry jam. Merry Christmas and Happy New Year to everyone."

Jamal P. shared a Muslim Christmas in Istanbul at the grand bazaar, checking out Aya Sofia, the former mosque-turned-museum, "amid the wondering fully-covered women and worshippers, prostrating themselves to Allah, near the shrines, nestled deep, walking the crowded square where taxis careened, outnumbering other vehicles ten-to-one. A sole farmer emerges, holding the reins of two camels as he tries to pass them off as reindeers with antlers, bells, and everything."

Michael D. remembered himself and his wife "taking a ride on our 1948 74-inch original Harley hog through luscious green mountain countryside, with a touch of snow on the side of a long winding road, feeling the cold crisp air biting at our faces."

Midget Porn ended our makeshift Christmas celebration by taking a humorous tilt, ending the class on a bawdy but positive note just when things were about to get a bit maudlin:

One Christmas Eve I came home late, stoned and cold. I pulled into the driveway and to the porch and I hear, "Pssst, excuse me, could you give me a hand?"

I looked up and there was Mrs. Claus up on the roof, looking down at me. I got the ladder from beside the house. When I made it up, Mrs. Claus informed me that her husband was drunk and she was driving this night. Her husband was stuck in my chimney. Could I help her? I helped her get her old man out. Yeah, he was drunk alright. He passed smooth out when we got him back in the sleigh. I told Mrs. Claus, "Jeez, it was nice to meet you ma'am."

"Likewise I'm sure," she said. "And to show my appreciation, I'm gonna give you a hand job."

Well, it sure was the best hand job I ever had . . . and also the bestest Christmas ever.

That class was "the bestest" Christmas celebration we ever had, too. Later, in the years that followed, depending on which day the holidays fell, as well as if and when lockdowns occurred, our Christmas celebrations would vary. On more than one occasion, because of violence and lockdowns, we'd read back Christmas stories in mid-January, once the yard fell back into a dull routine. Nobody minded that Christmas happened in January. Behind the walls, time has a way of becoming increasingly ambiguous during holidays. Or as biker Ace succinctly wrote, "What is Christmas to a man in prison without his family and loved ones? Just another day."

CHAPTER 15:

My Favorite Things, Tattoos & Scars, and Lunch on Arnold

(Sung to the tune of the famous standard "My Favorite Things.")

"Skinheads and headbangers, Goths and hip-hoppers. OG's and rappers alongside beboppers . . . these are a few of my favorite things."

Because of our musical backgrounds, it was a treat to watch different shreds of music culture converge in our classroom sanctuary. Because of the transient nature of H-Unit, we were experiencing "the churn," a steady influx and departure of all types of inmates. We'd lose some of the best and the brightest, but then gain new faces and fresh writers.

Music was a solid staple for the guys doing time on the H-Unit yard. Inmates would wander in with their transparent clear plastic prison-built approved CD players, wearing their translucent headsets. With so many music lovers in the class, it was tempting to want to bring in burnt CD-R's of current and classic music selected from our extensive music collections at home, but that was technically a no-no. One tall gangly student we called Tall Paul was a fervent fan of Trent Reznor and Nine Inch Nails. At the time, coincidentally, we were collaborating with Reznor on the idea of doing a book. We spent hours sitting with him, though nothing came of it. Like us, Reznor hailed from a small town in Western Pennsylvania.

Tall Paul was a slim, good-looking kid, and a gifted writer. Long-haired. Well-read, but clinically and creatively Gothic dark. During the day, he would walk the perimeter of the yard almost trancelike with a detached stride. He wrote about his broken Southern California home life, and about how his father worked in a hospital. Every day after school, Paul would sit in the hospital waiting room until his father was off his shift, occupying himself by reading magazines, doing his homework amid patients awaiting treatment. A strange way to spend after-school hours.

Paul's creative writing was eerie and filled with explicit images of intravenous drug use, though he assured us that he'd never engaged in such activity. We believed him, because as versed as we were in motorcycle clubs and crime, we hadn't partaken of those lifestyles ourselves—proof that it's entirely possible to absorb certain aspects of popular culture without actually living them.

As we accumulated more class terms under our belts, we thought that maybe we should map out a more universal Creative Writing curriculum. In other words, put together a cohesive ten-week program based on tried-and-true writing subjects and lessons with a few variations. Back in our days at San Francisco State University, many professors had done just that. They developed a set curriculum, learned it backwards and forwards, and simply taught by rote semester after semester. It was a tempting academic proposition. Find six or seven of the most provocative writing subjects and assign them throughout the quarter, then reassign them again and again, throw in a few core lectures on the publishing biz, and voilà!, we have an instant canned Creative Writing class. Just add water. That was actually the original plan. Develop a teaching experience that would adapt to the college experience.

Easier said than done. Our writing topics needed to be fresh and current, tailored to each class's makeup and temperament. From time to time we repeated writing assignments and shared the previous writings with the class. But we could not succumb to the dull routine of teaching from a rigid curriculum. Besides, we were attracting what we jokingly called repeat offenders, that is, students doing long stretches of time who took our class over and over again. Even with the churn of new faces, it was more fun to keep things fresh and free-form and, in the process, accumulate a large list of cool writing topics.

Some of our best writing assignments came to us from out of the blue, sometimes at the very last minute as we crossed the Richmond San Rafael Bridge, minutes before hitting the San Quentin turnoff. But some of our best writing assignments required a little more thought. Example: My Favorite Things.

"My Favorite Things" is a well-known show tune from the 1959 Rodgers and Hammerstein musical, *The Sound of Music*, made famous on Broadway by Mary Martin and on-screen by Julie Andrews. Even the most hardcore hip-hoppers in our class knew the song from their elders. The lyrics are bright and chirpy, and the dichotomy of "raindrops on roses and whiskers on kittens" or "cream colored ponies and crisp apple strudels" read aloud against the backdrop of the stark H-Unit prison yard outside was too sardonic to resist. To compound the absurdity, we enlisted the biggest, most menacing-looking student in the class to stand up in front of the class and read the lyrics aloud. We picked a huge Samoan student to recite the lyrics with vigor and enthusiasm. Everybody caught the joke, but they also perceived the bittersweet spirit of Oscar Hammerstein's lyrics and how familiar lines and phrases could be reinterpreted as brand new.

Plus, it was a unique way of asking incarcerated students to ponder a valid subject: "What are a few of your favorite things?" For extra inspiration, we popped John Coltrane's rendition of "My Favorite Things" into the CD player of the class's television monitor.

The class wrote feverishly. Seeing three dozen San Quentin hep cats scribbling "their favorite things" to the free-jazz strains of Coltrane, McCoy Tyner, Jimmy Garrison, and Elvin Jones is a fond memory we cherish to this day.

The writing results were wide-ranging and inspired, milking all five senses—touch, taste, smell, sound, and sight—or, as William Shakespeare referred to them, "the five wits." Most of the descriptions were filled with longing, drawing from a wealth of personal experience.

One student named Morris P. interspersed his military experiences with an urban battlefield.

> Choppers in the sky, the sound, the perfect formation, or just a single chopper flying around at different angles, hovering or flying straight ahead. Choppers revving up and taking off. Choppers landing lightly on the ground. Machine guns, handguns, shotguns, the feel of them, the sound, the accuracy. The fun of blowing the hell out of things and the smell of the powder.

Marvin A. covered a wide spectrum of secular images and religious contradictions.

> Raider games, breast milk, sex with my wife, children, muscle cars, Cal football, movies and making movies, hot bath, hearing my wife say she loves me, and the freaking Oakland A's, pork chops, James Brown music . . . but most of all, Jesus Christ. Seeking knowledge, watching porn, doing things people say I can't, family reunions, Oakland, California, pit bulls, volunteering at shelters, making people laugh, Will Ferrell movies, helping children learn how to write, watching my daughter dance, being an activist, networking, making deals, money, candy (Mike & Ikes), going to church, carnivals, playing basketball, cutting hair, watching PBS, dreaming of freedom.

Bobby F. took the crown with an eclectic "My Favorite Things" list, diving into the past and present.

The frosting bowl when I was a kid. Mom's hugs. My cat's attitude. '60s muscle cars. The wind in my face. Lightning in the middle of New Mexico at night. Mae West on the *Mike Douglas Show* or any talk show. My wife's head on my chest when she's sleeping, listening to her breathe and feeling her heartbeat. The Grand Canyon. Taking drives on curving roads like Highway One. Sitting in restaurants with my girl, people watching and putting people together and laughing at what their offspring would look like. Standing on the corner asking people directions to see if they know where they are. Barbequing on my back porch. Listening to the music of the ocean waves. Going to concerts in Golden Gate Park. Playing computer games with my girl, online together. Watching someone rushing on meth. Skipping rocks across the pond or lake. Drinking out of mountain creeks. Eating or watching people eat. Racing on Mulholland Drive. The different colored sands in the Philippines: white, black, red, and gray.

Howie B. offered a travelogue description of the Painted Desert.

One of my favorite things is walking in the Arizona desert after a typical summer rain. I love the way the thunderheads build up over the mountains in the afternoons of the hot July and August days. The way there is rhythm to the storms as they build and build in the stillness and then unleash on the mountain before moving across the valley and towards the south. It's nice to stand just inside shelter where you can see and inhale the desert after its rebirth. All of the plants and animals seem to perk up and revel in the purified air. As the day moves toward sunset, the sky is God's canvas. The horses and jackrabbits graze side by side while the mesquites soak up the precious moisture. The best part is the way it smells like dirt and how nature seems to come out to enjoy it together. When you go out through the parched arroyos that have run after being dry for weeks or months, you get to see the *javelinas* gather to drink and the rattlesnakes come back out to sun on the warm pavement. There's no better way to see a sunset and experience the Arizona desert.

The guys were delving deep. Writing on demand, using the five wits, is a difficult exercise. We liked to compare it to laying down a vocal track in the recording studio and nailing it on the first take. By this time, we were no longer surprised by the depth and quality of the guys' writing.

Another colorful writing subject in our assignment repertoire was "Tattoos & Scars." It's a subject that draws multileveled response, graphic tales of scars, physical or mental, ranging from a burn mark from a taser, an ice pick puncture, twenty minutes of searing, excruciating pain getting "branded" with a white hot poker, or the emotional shot of pain coming from receiving a Dear John letter from the wife or "old lady." Whenever we threw out "Tattoos & Scars" as a writing assignment, a lot of pain came hurtling back at us. But nobody hit it out of the park quite like Big Bob, who wrote:

> Tattoos & Scars.
> The question after every arrest, while they are booking you:
> "Do you have any scars, marks or tattoos?"
> Yeah.
> Left cheek of my ass. Burn marks from a taser in County. Punk ass cop sprayed me with a water hose first, and that was the time I learned it truly is their world.
> Two scars on my back. Two scars on my chest, left elbow, and hands. Nine times the knife went in before I threw his punk ass off the tier. The cop in the tower told me later he was about to shoot me as I ran down the stairs. He thought I was going

after the dude who flew off the tier, but then he realized I was running toward the cop shack. With nine holes in you, would you have run anywhere else?

Left leg. Huge Z-shaped scar. Cut my leg with a razor. Packed the wound with my own feces. Needed to get an infection to go to the outside hospital for a contact visit with my gal. Four days later, I wake up, a doctor drawing on my leg with a grease pencil, telling another doctor how the amputation would go. I grab his throat and scream,

"Don't take my leg!"

He tries antibiotics for thirty minutes. White cell count goes down enough to continue treatment.

I keep my leg.

Won't try that again although the contact visits were kinda worth it.

One day after dropping by the H-Unit yard for a teachers' meeting, Kent noticed it was chow time. Lunch on the H-Unit yard! We wondered about the food at H-Unit. After meeting a group of students on the yard, Kent ambled into the food line with the rest of the guys. The CO policing the line let Kent pass into the chow hall. He looked at his three students, Ace the Biker, Donnie the Kid, and Eric G. the ex-junkie and suddenly realized: Wow! A prison lunch courtesy of Governor Arnold Schwarzenegger!

Amid the numerous complaints we heard about prison food, here was a golden opportunity to blow the story wide open: exactly how bad *was* the food inside the H-Unit chow hall? While we'd already been inside there for Town Hall meetings and our sponsored Ice Cream Social, here was Kent's chance to sample the prison cuisine. He grabbed a tray and walked across the food line behind Ace, Donnie, and Eric, after which the four grabbed an empty table and dug in for chow.

Since the feedings were organized dorm by dorm within a compressed amount of time, the process was remarkably precise and well organized. But the cuisine was also respectable! Stringy beef burrito, Spanish rice, refried whole beans, and an ice cream sandwich washed down with iced tea. Not as tasty as the 20th Century Fox commissary in Los Angeles, but not too shabby. H-Unit food was surprisingly splendid considering it was prison food. While Burrito Day at SQ wasn't exactly five-star Michelin French cuisine, it wasn't as inedibly as the men had described it. It was far better than the bagged lunches of flattened baloney sandwiches, rubbery carrots, and broken crackers or cookies served inside county jail.

CHAPTER 16

Big Bob and Flying under the Radar

Big Bob slinked through the classroom door a few minutes early before we were formally announced over the public address system. He sneaked a couple of football slips to us. It was midway through the NFL season and Bob's H-Unit football pool was in full operation. After the early Vegas line hit the sports pages every Tuesday, Big Bob scored access to the copy machine. He printed and distributed his miniature tags throughout the yard, which paid out in tobacco pouches and postage stamps rather than cold cash. Big Bob let us play and not once did we come close to winning. But even if lightning had struck twice and we had won, our winnings of tobacco and stamps would have been recycled back into "the house." Predictably, the week after Super Bowl Sunday and the Pro Bowl, when football season ended, Big Bob would recess into a deep depression and funk.

Like Red, Morgan Freeman's character in *The Shawshank Redemption,* Bob was really wired into the system, so we asked him to spot-check something for us. A few weeks prior we had dropped off a set of the books we had written and donated them to the San

Quentin/H-Unit lending library. After getting many requests from students wanting to read our stuff, we decided to tough out the paperwork trail, fill out the donation forms, and give the inmates access to our literary body of work. We figured Big Bob could find out if the books had been received and processed into the library. When we brought up the subject to follow up, Bob just shook his head. The news was not good.

"Guys," he said, "the books aren't here. Not in H-Unit, anyway. How long has it been since you brought them in?"

"Musta been three weeks ago," Kent estimated, grimacing. "I lugged those damn things in myself at the last education meeting. Two shopping bags full of books. We gave them to the clerk for him to process with all the right donation forms filled out. Now they're gone? How can that be?"

"I have no doubt they made it inside okay," Bob replied. "Maybe they went uphill to the main library, or they were 'intercepted' along the way."

Intercepted? After asking around a little more, it became apparent that our entire literary gift had taken a mysterious detour and was not to be seen again. Nobody from the class could read our works—including our newest book, a collection of essays about modern American roots rock music, entitled *Sing My Way Home*. The book sported a snazzy cover featuring Gram Parsons strumming a vintage Gibson dreadnought guitar.

Rather than make a big stink about it, we moved on. While it was frustrating, we decided it wouldn't be wise to stir up any trouble by demanding an explanation. Besides, life at SQ was easier for us flying under the radar every Friday night.

At the next class we were greeted with more bad news. We'd lost one of our "Bigs"—Big Head had been sent to the Hole. He'd slipped us "a kite" through another inmate. A kite is a tightly folded paper message that's passed from cell to cell. We opened the tightly compressed message to find that Big Head had written us a short paragraph on what it was like to be in solitary confinement. He delved into the excruciating boredom of no one to talk to and harrowing uncertainty of solo incarceration, and how time had lost its frame of reference, which had a dizzying effect on his head and psyche. Upon reading it, Keith scratched his head. It was a well-written piece, to be sure—and a viable souvenir of the class to show to friends. But maybe it wouldn't be a good idea to leave the grounds with it on our person. We were being paranoid, but what if it were intercepted and perceived as some coded message? Keith dropped the kite into the wastebasket. Later on, according to the gossip mill, after leaving Ad Seg, Big Head would be transferred to another state prison after being caught in possession of confidential records of members of H-Unit's inmate population.

From teaching the class, we liked to think that we were fairly street-smart and pretty good judges of character. We could tell rather quickly if we were being bullshitted or taken for a ride. But one area where we may have been a little green was the druggie angle. We don't knowingly fraternize or hang out with high alcoholics, dope fiends, or heavy drug users, and if we have, then they've done a damn good job of hiding their excesses and abuse. The same was true in our class. If someone was getting high or walking into Creative Writing feeling fine on Cloud Nine (on a substance not administered in the Hot Meds line), it wasn't always something we'd pick up on right away. Such was the case with Eli. Eli sat in the back corner of the class every week nodding his head, with a perpetual crinkly grin on his face. While we had an idea what kind of sugar-plum fairies were dancing around in Eli's head, we were more interested in the fact that Eli liked to write about hitting the Northern California back roads on his rice rocket motorcycle.

In dealing with incarcerated men, the hardest concept for us to wrap our heads around was the anomaly of someone getting thrown into a prison in an area close to where they'd lived or grown up. For example, it must be maddening for a Chicago Outfit gangster accustomed to the finest Italian restaurants and swinging nightclubs in the Windy City to be arrested and confined to a dreary cell at the Metropolitan Correctional Center (MCC), a multistoried federal holding facility located right in the center of downtown Chicago!

It's one thing to serve a stretch on Terminal Island or in some arid Central California hellhole town like Avenal, amidst the fruited plains of the corporate agricultural belt, but quite another matter to do a multiyear hitch at San Quentin, situated in pastoral and terminally mellow Marin County—especially if that's where you grew up. How weird it must feel to have friends and family going about their everyday lives in the same region where you're locked down for years.

One Friday, in conjunction with a lesson we taught on writing photo captions and including pictures with a manuscript, we brought in a copy of our book, *Soul on Bikes,* to pass around as a visual aid. It demonstrated the use of four-color picture placement, including photographic "endpapers," i.e., the inside facing cover pages of a hardbound book. By the end of class, when it was time to reclaim the book, the inevitable request came up.

"Can't you just leave us the book?" they pleaded.

A dozen anxious hands shot up from students willing to take the volume off our person. Quite often we were asked to sign dog-eared copies of our books that had been sent to inmates via Amazon and subsequently passed around the H-Unit yard. But this was different.

That night we must have taken our stupid pills. Perhaps we were irritated that our donated books had been swiped by some cagey jailbird in the SQ library, or that it had been awhile since we'd raffled off the last of the signed Orange County Chopper placards. What the hell, Kent tugged off his vintage Guns N' Roses cap and walked around the full classroom.

"Okay! Write your name on a slip of paper and toss it in the hat. Whoever wins promises to share and pass the book around to the other guys. Big Bob, you come up and draw the lucky winner."

Bob stuck his hand inside the baseball cap, mixed up the contents, and emerged with a winning slip of paper. He grinned as he read the scrawled name.

"Eli!"

Eli ambled up to the front to collect his prize. His crinkly grin had grown to a toothy smile as he pumped his fist in the air. As the crowd exited the room, Eli gleefully handed us back the book.

"Can you guys sign this for me?"

Satisfied that a deserving writer, much less a devoted bike rider, had won the prize, we scribbled our monikers in the book:

Best Wishes to Eli . . .

Respectfully, Keith Zimmerman and Kent Zimmerman

A few weeks later, our phone rang at our writing compound. It was SQ Sinead, the education coordinator for the Success Program. Kent picked up the phone.

"Listen, are you guys coming into the prison for your class tonight?" she asked.

"Sure. What's up?"

"I'm not quite sure, but the lieutenant from the third shift wants to speak with you and your brother."

"Really?"

"Something to do with a book one of the inmates had. I'm not sure what's going on, but I wanted to give you a heads up about it anyway."

Uh-oh. Not a good thing when custody demands an audience.

That Friday, as we signed in at the H-Unit security gate at dusk, the CO on duty immediately picked up his phone and dialed out. "The writing teachers have just come in," he said, and slammed the receiver down.

"The lieutenant needs to speak to the two of you in the watch commander's office. He's there waiting for you."

Having gotten the warning call from SQ Sinead, we weren't

altogether shocked that we were being summoned to speak to the officer in charge of the third shift. We took two seats in his office, housed behind glass windows instead of solid walls. We had not yet met the gray-haired officer sitting behind the desk. His predecessor, an amiable guy who was a Harley-Davidson rider, had shown us snapshots of a cross-country bike ride he had taken. Like us, he was a big fan of Chris Cornell's Soundgarden spin-off band, Audioslave. Unfortunately, he had been transferred up to North Block, and something told us the new lieutenant facing us hadn't summoned us to his office to talk about heavy metal music or Harleys.

"It's come to our attention," he told us, "that a certain inmate in Dorm 5 has received an unauthorized hardbound book from the two of you." He pulled out our *signed* copy of *Soul on Bikes.*

Oh shit. We exchanged nervous glances. Eli had screwed up. And we'd just been caught red-handed. Our signatures were on the front page of *SOB,* personally inscribed to Eli. There was nothing else to do but 'fess up—and be *deeply* apologetic.

"Yes, Lieutenant," Kent said, "we did give that book to an inmate, and for that we apologize. We know it's against the rules."

"It was a one-time thing," Keith continued. "And we promise not to do it again. It was a careless mistake on our part, and we regret it."

We skulked out of the office, half embarrassed and half wondering what the hell was going to happen to us in the future. Would we be joining our H-Unit comrades out on the yard dressed in CDCR blues? During the class that night we were tightlipped about the incident, and Eli was noticeably absent on the sign-in sheet. One of his bunkie classmates confirmed to us after class that he had been sent to the Hole for disciplinary reasons. Why weren't we surprised?

At the end of class, we motioned for Big Bob to stick around. The first thing you noticed about Bob were his striking blue eyes and his close-cropped prematurely gray hair. Instead of the regulation blue work shirt and denim jeans, Bob wore a floppy gray sweat-shirt and a pair of blue track shorts, which made him look more like a high school gym teacher than a convicted two-strike felon.

"Dude," Kent said to Bob. "We just got called into the lieutenant's office before class tonight. They busted us."

"I know," Big Bob said knowingly. "I heard about it."

Of course. Nothing happened on the H-Unit yard that Big Bob didn't know about.

"What'd you guys say to the lieutenant?"

"We copped to it," Keith said. "We said we were sorry. What else could we do?"

Bob nodded his head. "Good move."

Turned out, according to Big Bob, Eli had been rousted out of his bunk. They'd searched through his locker and thrown out all of his stuff. They'd found the book we'd given him, and inside they'd found, let's put it this way . . . certain contraband.

"Oh damn," we sighed in unison. "What kind of stuff?"

"Drug stuff."

"Oh shit."

"The cops grabbed the book and saw Sonny Barger's name on the front cover and asked him where he got it. It didn't take a mental giant to figure out where it came from after you guys had signed it to Eli."

Bob continued, "All week, the word on the yard was that your class was done. The cops were pissed off! I heard that they called up to the Education office on the hill and asked about you guys. They wanted to know if they were aware of your affiliation with motorcycle gangs."

"And?"

"Education told custody they had already known about you, and that they had signed off on you guys teaching here. But in the meantime, the guys were pretty bummed out because they had grounds to cancel your class. The word was out. You guys were toast."

Oh no.

Then Bob cracked his trademark boyish, charming smile. "So I went in and spoke to the lieutenant. I told him how important the class was to the men, and how much we look forward to it every Friday.

"I'm what you call a MAC, a Men's Advisory Committee representative," said Bob, pointing out at the yard. "That means I'm part of an inmate committee that deals with issues between custody and the H-Unit population. I told the lieutenant that if he would let us keep our writing class and give you guys a pass, I'd help make sure we don't have problems with the white guys and the other folks out on the yard."

Holy shit! Big Bob had saved our sorry asses. From what we could gather, the class had been hanging by a thread due to our own carelessness and stupidity. Had it not been for Big Bob, we would have been escorted out of the gate, our class cancelled, and our good intentions tossed to the wind. It was fortunate that we had submitted our books in our first meeting with Ms. Bracy. Nobody likes surprises, especially in prisons.

We learned a valuable lesson that day, though it wouldn't be the last time we'd end up on the wrong end of a prison administration desk. CDCR rules are strict, and are sometimes moving targets, too. What's tolerated one week is frowned upon the next. What we learned was that no matter how long we walked the line, there was the possibility of tripping up and finding ourselves in trouble again.

By the next week, it was back to normal. We were teaching again, and Eli got out of the Hole. They even gave him his book back.

CHAPTER 17

The Broken Nose Bandit

When you're locked down, the most minor of occurrences—even those over which you have no control—can become major ordeals that affect your life profoundly. Take, for example, tobacco consumption in the California prison system. Once upon a time it was legal to smoke cigarettes in San Quentin. Tobacco pouches were issued along with basic cosmetics like soap or shampoo inside "fish kits." Largely responsible for this was Clinton T. Duffy, reputedly the greatest warden that San Quentin ever had (and author of *88 Men and 2 Women*, which influenced us greatly as young readers). An early advocate of rehabilitation within the state correctional system, Duffy distributed tobacco pouches (complete with rolling papers) free of charge to prisoners during his term as warden between 1940 and 1952. As a result, SQ pouches were briefly nicknamed "Duffy tobacco." But on July 1, 2005, Governor Arnold Schwarzenegger put on the brakes and declared tobacco consumption to be unlawful inside a CDCR facility—just as authorities had previously banned working out with free weights. San Quentin became a smoke-free institution.

Inmates used to purchase tobacco at the canteen. The canteen is actually the commissary window where the men buy all their incidentals to get them through their weeks. Snack foods like Top Ramen soup mixes, coffees, teas, hot chocolate, candy bars, salted snacks, beef salami sticks, and sundries like shampoos, soaps, shaving cream, plastic razors, Mennen's Speed Stick, and toothpaste, postage stamps in packages up to 40, and batteries are all available for purchase upon appointment. It's a common occurrence on the H-Unit yard to see an inmate walking back to his barracks with one of those large netted bags elderly women in Chinatown carry around, filled with his personal essentials.

(One thing we wondered: beyond the requisite three square meals a day, the three pairs of underwear, socks, two pairs of pants and two shirts that are laundered every ten days, how much exactly does it take to live large in prison? According to a small sample of inmates we questioned, at least $200 a month dumped into an inmate's canteen account could easily put him in the upper percentile of prison wealth.)

By April 2005, CDCR prison authorities preempted the tobacco prohibition by banning the sale of "pouches" in the H-Unit canteen three months prior to the official ban taking effect. So by July, once the ban had taken place, naturally tobacco pouches became a molten hot prison commodity. The pouch, previously perceived as simple prison yard currency, was dubbed the new gold standard, where the going rate for a seemingly innocent $1.45 bag of roll-your-own, low rent Bugler Tobacco skyrocketed. Prices for a pouch that provided convict smokers with .65 ounces of leaf, enough to make approximately three dozen pinner-styled cigarettes, affectionately called "bindles" out on the H-Unit yard, soared. The tobacco ban changed life inside San Quentin twofold. Suddenly the air got easier to breathe, and also as an old form of legitimate currency was banned a new underground currency was born.

Prior to the July ban, many of our savvy classmates had stockpiled pouches for the not-too-distant future when desperate, strung out nicotine addicts would pay almost anything for an illicit puff. For many smokers, their only resort was to kick cigarettes cold turkey, since nicotine patches and other prescribed remedies were not permitted within the prison walls—especially nicotine gum, which could be used to jam up locks in an aged facility like Q. One inmate opted to convert to Buddhism and begin meditating in a last ditch spiritual attempt to kick the habit.

It didn't take a rocket scientist to ascertain that when cigs became illegal in California prisons, new clandestine smuggling operations would sprout up overnight. Crooked CO's, family visitors, state highway maintenance crew personnel and bad apple convicts were poised and ready to form new unholy and lucrative alliances to supply a steady stream of smokes to the prison yards, including H-Unit.

So how does the illicit supply of tobacco find its way onto the yards? There are a few possible sources. Since tobacco is a legal stimulant on the outside, bringing it inside isn't conceived of as a crime as serious as sneaking in illegal drugs, prescriptions, or paraphernalia, so it's relatively easy for it to just be brought in. Then another source is confiscated tobacco that's recycled back onto the yard.

It was a hot Friday when everyone on the yard, including CO's and administrators, was required to hand over their smokes. Men crazy for a cigarette rifled through their personal belongings, desperately looking for something to sell to secure a nicotine fix. The ban pitted friend against friend, bunkie against bunkie. With the hiding places available around the prison grounds, enforcement detection efforts resembled a large-scale Easter egg hunt. While some inmates groused philosophically about having to endure yet another freedom taken away, we were unfazed. Being nonsmokers, we had already eliminated the midway smoke break from our class simply because some wise guys would duck out of class after an assignment and not come back.

Near the start of class that July night, Big Bob grabbed an ink marker and listed on the whiteboard the latest ongoing prices for illicit pouches, which we laughingly referred to as "the SQ Pouch Commodities Index." It was your typical frenzied prohibition scenario. Pouches available at any convenience store for $1.50 shot up into the $20 range by the end of the first week. As we approached and passed the two-week mark, pouches hit $50 and surged toward $60 apiece. One commodity-wise student couldn't wait any longer. He began liquidating his pouches for gold and silver jewelry. Six cigarettes could fetch an inmate's wedding band.

We heard that on July 2nd, when tensions were running high in and around the dorms, personal ash trays began mysteriously disappearing. One person was caught stealing tobacco out of an inmate's locker. It proved to be bad news for the tobacco thief because when the cops left the dorm area, he was confronted by four fellow inmates. After they severely battered and bruised him, each inmate took an arm and a leg and tossed the culprit out of the dorm barracks front door. Exhausted and weak from an ass-kicking, the unfortunate convict slid face first across the asphalt, adding road rash to his list of injuries.

In response to the new law, we did what any self-respecting, opportunistic creative writing teacher would do: we made it a writing assignment entitled "The Year Tobacco Left San Quentin." For the protection of our students, and to insure anonymity, we deleted the names from each entry. One tongue-in-cheek black inmate used the topic as a vehicle to mix sensuality and satire that would have made Barry White nod his head with approval.

I've been waiting all day to have you against my lips. The taste. The smell of you has been driving me crazy. It's insane to have you on my arm when I know everyone around wants a piece of you. Oh yeah, baby, daddy can't wait to kiss you, make love to you like it's the last time on earth. We got a love that will last. "I'm the fire and you are the desire." Ain't that what Rick James said? I hope my bunkie don't get his ass up, 'cause I'm not sharing you with nobody. This is love, baby, can't you tell, girl? I'm gonna suck on you like a barbeque rib. A "115" [violation] ain't got shit on the way you make me feel. I'll go to hell and back just to be with you. Come here, girl. It's time to make love.

We didn't bother to ask Big Bob if he was involved in speculating on the SQ Pouch Commodities Index. Actually, with the elimination of pouches, Bob had lost one of his primary legitimate currencies (besides cash, soups, and postage stamps) for his NFL pool operation. Then, not long after the prison environment had acclimated itself to the smoking prohibition and the tobacco frenzy had died down, Big Bob was given something much more precious: his release papers to leave San Quentin, after serving 38 months inside.

After his first stint inside the CDC system, Big Bob had earned a degree in chemical engineering. Later diagnosed as bipolar, and with depression issues and suicide running in his family, Big Bob had hit the crack pipe hard and took a careless swing at a drug dealer, fatally knocking him down onto the concrete sidewalk. Before we knew him, Big Bob had already served eight years for that manslaughter charge. We crossed paths while he was doing a stretch at H-Unit on a shoplifting beef (two packs of cigarettes from a convenience store) that required him to serve, according to California's strict Three Strikes sentencing laws, eighty percent of another mandatory four-year sentence.

Within months of his release from San Quentin, Bob opened a small but thriving Haz Mat—hazardous waste material—inspection business that dealt with corporate hazardous waste like mold and chemical spills. So we again broke a long-standing rule and reached out to a former student as a friend. Shortly after his release, we took Big Bob to an NBA game. We sat fifteen rows from courtside to watch the Golden State Warriors battle the Portland Trailblazers, ironically known at the time as the "Jailblazers" because of some

players' dalliances with possession of weed and assault and battery
punch-ups.

The game was quite a spectacle for a newly released ex-con
who had spent his last four years cooped up in the close quarters of H-Unit. Superhero NBA stars slammin' and jammin'
the rock to the rim. Miniature blimps flying overhead. Balled
up T-shirts shot into the crowd with bazooka-type air cannons
dropping prizes. A live funk band on a balcony stage. Hot pizza
boxes flung into the crowds at halftime. Stunned and in awe,
Big Bob leaned over to us after a legion of gorgeous Warrior
Girls converged at center court during a time-out, kicking their
legs high and shaking their shapely booties.

"Don't tell the guys inside, but I really like the black one over
there," he confided.

It was a kick to see Bob function as a civilian; we found him to
be a kid at heart. We watched his eyes widen as the souvenir ven-
dor trolled up and down the coliseum stairs. He stuffed himself on
churros and cotton candy.

By then, Bob had entered into a career fast lane. Within
a few months following his release from incarceration, Bob
already had four full-time employees working at his Haz Mat
venture. He dutifully paid his workers' comp, SSI, FICA, and
quarterly tax estimates, and within a matter of months had developed a small but impressive list of Silicon Valley clients including a well-known international brewer and distiller of a
lineup of prominent alcoholic brands of tequila, whiskey, and
beer who had just encountered a serious chemical spill. Bob
had enrolled his children into pricey private Christian schools,
lavished the family with gifts, and flown them on cross-country
trips. A wise parole officer visited his home. He took one look
at Big Bob's business balance sheets and soundly warned him.

"Be careful. You're moving way too fast."

Bob was soldiering through each day on heavy doses of medical marijuana and Wellbutrin. Then, the same year the Wall Street brokerages began to hemorrhage, his business and personal life unraveled. His small business encountered cash flow problems, and soon his bankers and creditors decided to reel him in. Big Bob was bleeding cash and his lines of credit were called in. He was ordered to pay up within the next ten days. So Big Bob did what any cagey, street-smart H-Unit inmate might do.

He started robbing banks.

To satisfy his bank creditors, Bob bought a wig, hat, glasses, and a toy gun and went to work. He hit a large chain bank for $6,000, and within the next 12 days, he hit eleven more financial institutions, scoring an impressive grand total of $176,000.

A couple months before his bank robbing spree, Keith paid Big Bob a visit. By then he had left his wife and two children and moved into a run-down tract home with trailers and heavy equipment scattered across the front yard. The house was barely furnished, and Big Bob had fallen from living a tidy heroic suburban existence with his happy family to crashing on a pull-out futon in a bedroom-turned-office. His new pad felt more like a halfway house than a home, with ex-cons and vagabond roommates hanging about the place. Big Bob and Keith found an In-N-Out burger joint down the road in which to catch up and talk.

"So, what's with you splitting up with your family?"

Big Bob sighed, and then he perked up. His kid-like demeanor returned. "It's true. But I did meet this foxy Latin chick down at the dry cleaners. Last week I brought her along to Parents Night at the Christian school I send my kids to. When my ex-old lady saw her with me, she freaked."

"You really think that was such a good idea?"

Bob was not playing with a full deck, but he swore he was clean and sober. Except that his parole officer, on a surprise second visit, discovered him drinking from a quart bottle of Budweiser. On the long drive home, Keith dialed Kent on the mobile phone.

"Man, I just left Big Bob's place. Things aren't looking too good."

February 29, 2008. We ran into Big Bob's buddy, Big Jon, out on the H-Unit yard—it was his second time back. At six-foot-three and 260 pounds, Jon was a bear of a white guy with tousled wavy brown hair and a moustache. Built like a left tackle, Big Jon owed the state a few more months and had gotten "violated" when his PO (parole officer) in the Napa Valley got back a dirty piss test. Back at Quentin, Big Jon aced his way through "reception," where he was issued an oversized orange jumpsuit and then was processed, examined, and dumped back into H-Unit dressed again in blues, where he scored his usual lower bunk in the back corner of Dorm One. While it was a bummer to see him return, we were secretly pleased to pencil Big Jon's CDC and bunk number back into our writing lineup—which is the niggling paradox we face whenever a student, particularly a good writer, returns to captivity. Nice to see you; sorry to see you.

Big Jon had a worried look on his face when class convened that Leap Year Friday night. Yet at the same time, he couldn't wait to give us the bad news. Word spreads lightning fast on a prison yard.

"Did'ja hear what happened?"

"No, what?" we asked.

"When you get home, type in 'Broken Nose Bandit' on the Google. You'll see."

"Holy shit!" Kent screamed at the computer screen later that night at home. A suspect dubbed by press and the police as the Broken Nose Bandit was staring back at us. According to the online news source, the bandit had allegedly knocked off five banks in the southern San Jose area. (One was a credit union while the rest posted FDIC signs on the front door, which carried an automatic 24-year federal sentence.) Along with the story of the bank jobs, the newspaper Web site included a security camera image of the robber's close-up mug. The face poking out of a hoodie was unmistakable.

"It's Big Bob!"

By February's end in 2008, Big Bob had robbed a bank across the street from the San Jose Police Department and netted another $47,000. During his spree of bank robberies, Bob had made three costly mistakes: First, the banks he had knocked off were within a five-mile radius of his residence and office. Second, he didn't use a disguise for his last robbery. Third, Big Bob had slipped back into smoking crack.

The morning after his final heist, Big Bob parked outside of a 7-Eleven near his home to drink a cup of coffee and read the morning newspaper, only to look back at a picture of himself underneath the headline "Broken Nose Bandit Strikes Twice in 24 Hours." Big Bob had earned his press-given nickname after nervously suffering a nosebleed during one of the stick-ups. His portrait, snapped by a high tech security cam, was clear as day. Any friend or relative would recognize him immediately. At that instant a police car pulled into the 7-Eleven parking lot right next to him. Looking over at the car, Bob saw the picture from the newspaper taped to the dashboard of the squad car! When the patrolman gazed over at Bob sitting in his vehicle, he approached him, asking his name and demanding he step out of the automobile. After the suspect was described as a white male of average height, Big Bob was tackled, handcuffed, and arrested. A search of his car produced a wad of cash (over thirty grand) plus a 33-gram stash of crack. Big Bob was in deep, deep shit.

The day after Bob was apprehended, the police obtained a search warrant and headed over to where Big Bob's wife and kids lived. Over a dozen family members were visiting for a family funeral. "Look!" yelled one of the youngsters who walked into the kitchen waving the newspaper, "Uncle Bob's picture is in the paper!" Seconds later, pandemonium broke out in the household as the cops entered and searched the premises. At the same time, Bob was taken into custody in the Santa Clara county jail and put on suicide watch.

Ten months later, we received an e-mail message from Big Bob through a mutual friend. The friend had scanned a letter from Bob in jail, handwritten in pencil on a yellow legal pad. After nearly a year bunked up in county, his trial hadn't started. His robbery spree, complete with gun possession and false imprisonment charges, constituted a third-strike offense. Big Bob was looking at a minimum of centuries of time. According to his friend, he was no longer the buffed up, confident, blue-eyed poster boy for the SQ Success Program that we remembered. Loaded up on bipolar meds, Bob was on his second public defender desperately fighting his case. He specifically asked for us to send a letter of support to the judge vouching for his character.

It was a tough and torturous decision, but after serious debate, we had to reluctantly and painfully cut him loose. Robbing several banks was a bizarre cry for help. Big Bob had chosen the path of recidivism and drug and drinking excess. Again. If we relented and "brought the street into our homes," becoming involved with the plight of every ill-fated character like Big Bob, what good would we be doing? We needed to draw the line, to stay solely on the teaching course, and keep an objective distance. The reality of our mission dictated staying focused and concentrating on the guys who were inside—otherwise we risked being dragged into the black hole of recidivism.

With the plight of Big Bob, we learned a difficult lesson firsthand: the world is a tough and unforgiving place, and with prison recidivism rates skyrocketing past 67 percent, brokenhearted souls like Big Bob who couldn't handle the overpowering stress of modern society would inevitably fall by the wayside. It takes a strong man to do hard time inside a state penitentiary. But it takes an even stronger one to stay afloat and free for the sake of his friends, family, and children, if not for himself. The question remained in our minds: would Big Bob and the Zimmermen cross paths again?

CHAPTER 18

Click Moment & The Tap Test

By April 2008, our fifth anniversary, the time had come for a jolt of outside input. As hired-gun writers, we were used to paving the road as we drove down it, often writing with little or no feedback from literary agents or editors prior to delivering a final manuscript. (Just do it!) Since we weren't credentialed teachers, nor were we experts in the fields of criminal behavior or rehabilitation, we wondered, how were we really doing? The class was growing. We were holding our audiences. Truth was, though, we harbored some self-doubt. Outside of Steve from the San Quentin arts department sitting in the back of the classroom for the first half of our very first class, we had been flying completely blind. Didn't school principles drop in unannounced on their teachers to check up on whether or not they were sticking to the program? Still, we appreciated the trust and freedom, and the opportunity to fly below the administrative radar.

Though we might not have had direct feedback, we had one thing going for us. The profession of writing has a mystique that fascinates folks—it's a craft that many hold in high regard. As a result, when any of our students saw themselves as potential writers and received reinforcement from us, then our class was a confidence builder to their character and to their writing skills. Miraculously, we had plucked some kick-ass scribes off the H-Unit yard, guys who would ordinarily be wasting away in their bunks doing nothing on a Friday night. Instead, we had them regurgitating their high-speed stories and inner thoughts and quite effectively articulating them on the blank page.

We were butts-in-seats showbiz guys who approached teaching as "putting on a show." Admittedly, we were sometimes guilty of being more concerned with keeping the inmates intrigued and entertained than we were with educating them. But in our limited and naïve philosophy as do-it-yourself professors, we hoped that our students were learning something important: that they were fully capable and worthy of sitting in any academic classroom once they were released. (Just do it!)

Still, we found ourselves stuck in a "forest for the trees" situation. As part of the H-Unit Success program, since we were neither fish nor fowl, we didn't quite fit the profile of teaching a self-help course. And ours was a far cry from the other classes that equipped the men with strong coping tools, like those teaching workshops about substance abuse, anger management, nutrition, and parenting. Conversely, our mantra was simply, "Once you get out, take a class, dammit! Stay off the streets on Friday nights and sit in a classroom." The question remained, was this effective? Were we getting our point across?

From the sidelines, we'd watched nearly a half-dozen San Quentin wardens come and go. One of them was Jill Brown, who retired in 2008 after spending a long career inside the CDCR but remained involved in helping to implement state policy in Sacramento. Working her way up from the state parole system to running San Quentin as a warden in 2004 and 2005, Jill was extraordinary in that, after leaving SQ as a public servant, she returned for a while to help supervise the H-Unit education program as a volunteer. Considering that the now-retired Jill is fifty-ish, with closely cropped, stylish red hair and a very feminine face, you'd be hard pressed to guess that this woman once put a man to death during her term as warden. After meeting her, we immediately requested a meeting with Jill to get some objective, professional feedback on our programming and education.

Over bags of chips and diet sodas, in the same snack bar where we'd met Ms. Bracy, with its million-dollar view of white-capped waves overlooking San Francisco Bay, we couldn't even throw out our first question before Jill led with one of her own.

"Have you guys noticed when someone in your class suddenly clicks and gets it? You see it in his face; it's a look in his eyes. Whether they're obtaining their GED or they're learning to write in a class like yours, almost out of nowhere, suddenly they get it. They decide to start learning and bettering themselves. 'I'm done with this prison stuff. I don't wanna come back.'"

That's when the concept of *Click Moment* dawned on us. Yeah, we'd seen it a few times, like when the smarter guys, hungry for intellectual exchange, stick around after class and talk incessantly about writing, film, and music.

Our motive for sitting with Jill was twofold. Was there any anecdotal or empirical evidence to show that we weren't the only ones getting something valuable out of those Friday nights? Besides having a good time, were we actually helping these guys? And were these classes putting the tiniest dent in the growingly grim incarceration and recidivism statistics? Who better to ask than a former warden? Few rehabilitation programs had the necessary funds to launch substantive research. In essence, as volunteers we were flying by the seats of our pants, crossing our fingers, and hoping we weren't merely wasting our days and nights teaching a bunch of knuckleheads.

"Well," said Jill, waving a piece of paper, "I just got this report from the CDCR saying that recidivism has dropped. Measured over a three-year period, overall recidivism was high at 67.5 percent. But the *one-year* recidivism rate has dropped from 49 percent to 46 percent. It's a small victory."

Then Jill threw out what we felt was an amazing statistic.

"Did you know that when an inmate is released and takes just *one* class like yours on the outside that the recidivism rate among even a part-time student drops in *ten percent* increments with each class they take? You're giving these guys an option to expand their minds. Remember, education wasn't encouraged in most of these guys' families."

Jill went on to point out that when our society and schools lose kids as young as six to ten years old to the streets, it's nearly impossible to reel them back into education mode. Instead, it's off to juvenile detention they go, with the taxpayers footing the bill for the remainder of their criminal careers. By programming inside San Quentin, was there a flicker of a chance they would rediscover the learning process and continue the educational process on the outside?

We asked Jill the important question that had been nagging us for months. Were we enlisting the most intelligent guys on the yard and just skimming the cream off the top? Or was the makeup of our class representative of the entire H-Unit criminal population? We suspected the former, but hoped for the latter. Jill, who had access to our attendance sheets and knew the criminal records of most of our H-Unit students, gave us a response that sort of shocked us.

"I'll just say this: you've got some pretty violent types with major street cred sitting in that classroom. Remember, your guys hang out on the yard just like they hang out on the street, so you are definitely attracting not just the usual student types, but I see a good cross-section of age, race, and social background."

Wow! Our snack bar conference with Jill was turning into a pep talk as our self-doubt dissipated. Turns out, according to Jill, we were attracting a cross-section of men that closely mirrored the demographics of the H-Unit yard. Not only were we reaching guys with a modicum of education, but we were also reaching guys who ordinarily wouldn't give a rat's ass about prison classes or education—like recruiting the black (and white) hip-hoppers, the young dudes who were fast becoming a strong contingent in our classroom. These writers viewed prison as a routine manly rite of passage, but often wrote hilarious vignettes about their off-the-hook adventures in South Central, Vallejo, Compton, Oakland's 69 Village, or the Vegas strip. Their stuff was often handwritten in elegant, cursive, calligraphic penmanship. Often times we didn't realize how rhythmic and syncopated their writing was until we actually read their pieces aloud for the first time in front of the class. These were students sporting gold teeth, wearing dreads, weaving tales of pimpin' and running drugs, barely a step ahead of the law and their gang-banging arch enemies on the street. Fascinating stuff.

Besides the young black writers, we were filling in a wide spectrum of other types of inmate students. Militant whites and skinheads, black and white OG's, hustler pimps, white hip-hopping Rage Against the Machine metalheads, Goths, Mexican street corner guys, bank robbers and burglars, gays, Native Americans, computer hackers, rednecks and peckerwoods, meth freaks, bikers, junkies, pot growers, serial drunk drivers, and, unbeknownst to us, violent offenders serving a maximum of up to ten years. At one point or another, these subcultures (for want of a better word) had passed through our classroom portals.

Damn! Our little class, "Finding Your Voice on the Page," was actually breaking down social barriers and crossing color lines. Because we were used to the wider racial spectrum of Northern California inmates, the only time we noticed the ethnic makeup of the class was when certain races were locked down because of fights, blood feuds, or other shenanigans. (We later learned that institutions in the Los Angeles area had an overwhelmingly larger Latino and black population than San Quentin.)

As Jill saw it, a black student could be attuned to the plight of the Mexican dude sitting next to him. Or the white student empathetic to what was going on in the mind of a Norteño or a Native American in the same room. By contrast, outside on the H-Unit yard, there was less open communication between the races. Guys usually stuck with their own. Yet inside the classroom, it wasn't unusual for an entire class—blacks, whites, Mexicans, "others"—to erupt in praise or applaud each other. If someone struck a poignant chord with their writing, a silence would hover over the room. Suddenly there was understanding (and even compassion) for somebody outside of an inmate's own racial boundaries.

What felt good was that we knew the unwritten rules: a white man sharing an illegal smoke with a Mexican was verboten. Same with a hot meds pill taken from a black man that couldn't be sold or passed off to a white man. And that there was someone watching you in case you failed to follow a racially motivated order, resulting in a beating from your own kind. These are only some of the constraints and demands that convicts live under.

"Older whites, young blacks, middle-aged Latinos," Jill said, "they're sitting in the same room, interacting with each other through their writing. You two may not realize it, but that's a new and powerful experience for many of these guys. And to be told by a writing professional that their stuff measures up, it's something they've never heard before.

"Taking your Creative Writing class—or programming, as the inmates call it—steers the men away from the negative influences, like the scammers and the so-called 'players' around them. You guys help give them focus and personal growth. Who else is giving them that?"

Turned out, we were offering a sanctuary of sorts, time away from the bully in the dorm or the petty prison gossip mill. The classroom had become a neutral zone, ranked alongside the chapel. Like church, the classroom was off-limits to violence and retribution.

The rule of the yard became: do not lean on a fellow inmate who is trying to better himself through education. We learned that the difference between religion and education behind bars was that religion was often left at the gate once an inmate was released whereas education traveled with him.

San Quentin was, comparatively speaking, an educational oasis in a dreary sea of state institutions. As proof, Jill passed us a copy of the *San Quentin News*. An inmate who had been transferred from SQ to a lower security lockup, CMC-West in San Luis Obispo—the same men's colony where Huey P. Newton and Timothy Leary did time—had had a letter published in the *SQ News*, the only inmate-written newspaper in the entire state penal system. (Yet another "plus" for San Quentin!)

"After last year's budget cuts in education," the inmate wrote, "there is nothing here [at CMC-West] for inmates to better themselves. It is a very stark comparison to what you guys have at SQ. . . . [so] feel blessed to be there, my friends, because I don't think there is a prison in the state that is so committed to positive programming as [San Quentin]."

That's when we experienced our Click Moment: maybe we should lighten up on ourselves and soldier on; maybe our little class was working, and maybe it even needed to be expanded to other institutions.

One of the advantages of team teaching was that we can seamlessly cover for each other. On rare ocassions one of us would teach the class alone. One such week, Kent was set to take over the class solo while Keith went on a brief holiday. As luck would have it, before Kent jumped into his wife's white Jeep Rubicon, he grabbed a few stray lesson plans and a copy of Jimi Hendrix's *Are You Experienced?*, which had just been reissued that week. Since the drive from Oakland to San Quentin during rush hour resulted in hellacious traffic,

Jimi singing "The Wind Cries Mary" might ease the pain of bumper to bumper congestion and cross-town traffic.

Rumbling down the back road to H-Unit, barely on time, with Jimi blasting away, Kent parked in the H-Unit lot and grabbed the lesson plans, but not before absentmindedly shoving the Hendrix CD into his jacket pocket. Upon entering H-Unit, Kent noticed an extra CO on duty at the sign-in.

"Empty your pockets," the officer ordered.

"No problem," said Kent, as he emptied his pockets. Pen. Erasable whiteboard marking pen. Car keys.

"Anything in your jacket pockets?"

Uh-oh. The Jimi Hendrix disc.

"What's this?"

"A Jimi Hendrix CD."

The CO, positioned as a sting operation to catch incoming cell phones, weapons, tobacco, and drug smugglers, had caught Kent red-handed—entering the H-Unit yard with a copy of *Are You Experienced?* in his jacket pocket. Not that there was anywhere inside to play the disc, mind you, except for the television DVD player, a paltry playback unit.

The CO pulled out an envelope and threw Jimi inside of it, scribbling Kent's name on the outside. He then wrote out a receipt. Technically, Jimi was considered contraband.

"You need to make an appointment with the warden if you want this back."

How stupid! Careless idiot! On his way out onto the yard, Kent's mind began to trip. Possession of a Jimi Hendrix CD could land him in one of the "dummy cages" that stood in the H-Unit watch station hallway. The dummy cage was where nasty inmates went as they were being written up for disciplinary infractions. The drill was that if any of the cages were occupied, you were forbidden to stare at the unfortunate inmate sitting inside. Kent checked his receipt. It read, in part:

"San Quentin State Prison Contraband Property Receipt. Contraband description: Music CD. Personal property identified as contraband will be returned directly to the employee by the Warden or Chief Deputy Warden. Employees will be required to make an appointment with the Warden's Secretary. Felonious contraband will not be returned and will be maintained in SQ Evidence pending disposition."

Was Jimi Hendrix "felonious contraband?" There was a time when he could have been.

The next day, Kent dialed the warden's office to make an appointment to rescue Jimi—and our reputations. A couple of days later, he found himself, head down, sheepishly entering the warden's office for the first time. It was sorta like being called to the principal's office, only ten times more humiliating.

The warden had a nice office. Not palatial, but sizable and prestigious-feeling. It was a gubernatorial appointed post. Kent greeted the warden, an affable guy nearly the same age as himself. After the two shook hands, they retired to the warden's personal conference room. Kent felt as if he'd just walked into *The Shawshank Redemption*.

"So," the warden asked, removing Jimi from the envelope, "what's this?"

"A Jimi Hendrix CD."

"What were you doing with it?"

"Listening to it on my way in from Oakland."

One thing about prison. If you're guilty, stupid, or both, you might as well cop to it.

"I take full responsibility," Kent said. "To be honest, I must have just shoved it into my pocket without realizing. I apologize."

The warden handed back the CD, along with a warning about smuggling in tobacco or cell phones. "Don't do it."

"Actually, I hate both tobacco *and* cell phones. Unfortunately, one of them is a necessity these days."

"What I do is the tap test," said the warden. "Before I enter a building here, I tap my pockets to make sure I'm not carrying something inside that I shouldn't. I advise you to be more careful because I will shut you down. I have nothing against cutting off my nose to spite my face."

"I understand," Kent answered timidly. After a moment of uncomfortable penance, he spoke up again. "Since I'm here, Warden, if you have a minute, can I tell you about our class?"

The warden checked his watch. "I have a few minutes. Fire away."

Kent told the warden the story of the class, piling on details about the impressive attendance and the miraculous writing. The warden nodded his head approvingly. Turned out to be a nice chap. Like the Z'men, he had attended San Francisco State University. He'd spent much of his career in public service. Then he expressed his appreciation for our taking the time and effort to teach the class. After a "few minutes" turned into 35 minutes, Kent asked one final question,

"So, how do you like being Warden of San Quentin? Truthfully."

The warden smiled. "Sometimes when I drive out of here, at the end of the day I feel like I've done some good work."

"What strikes me the most about San Quentin," Kent said, "is the whole love/hate thing. You hate this terrible place, but somehow, deep down, you love it, too. It's hard to explain to people who haven't been here."

"I know what you mean," the warden said, nodding his head. "I feel exactly the same way." Then he got up, shook Kent's hand and showed him to the door.

"Remember," the warden said, "tap test."

"Tap test," Kent repeated. "Thanks for talking to me. Good luck in keeping this place going."

Kent walked back out the East Gate toward his car, shed of embarrassment, with a spring in his step. Sure, he looked like an idiot getting busted for having Jimi Hendrix contraband in his pocket.

But then again, he'd seized the moment. Getting one-on-one face time with the warden of San Quentin State Prison wasn't easy. Being straight up was exactly the right thing to do. It felt good. On the drive out, Kent thought about Johnny Cash. Then Joe. They would have done the same. As the song goes, JC got jailed one night for picking flowers in Starkville, Mississippi. Kent wondered if Johnny Cash had heard about the tap test when he'd visited SQ. Then he laughed to himself.

The next week we received a frenzied call from our mum, Doris. "Joe just had a bad stroke this morning." Her voice cracked as she spoke. "He's in the ICU, unconscious."

CHAPTER 19

The Long Walk

Monday morning, February 2, 2009, Joe Zimmerman dutifully got up and made his and our mother's bed, after which he walked down the hall and into the kitchen to proudly announce,

"Honey, I made the bed for us."

After the words left his lips, a detached and eerie expression came over his ashen face, and he crumbled forward. He had been hit and felled by a massive stroke.

Those would be his last words.

Making the bed was a big deal for Joe, a symbolic act of both expressing gratitude to our mother for taking care of him and a declaration of his limited independence. Over the past months, Joe had become more and more depressed as his body grew weaker. He wasn't the type of fellow who took kindly to being cared for. Rather, he was accustomed to maintaining the household through a variety of practical around-the-house skills, the master fix-it guy with hundreds of tools hanging in his garage workshop. He kept the house we grew up in maintained and in good working order. In the past, he'd done the small things, like keeping the sprinklers and drainage systems of his yard in synchronicity while performing any minor electrical work that was required around the house. He changed his own oil on the front driveway. Whenever Joe saw something that needed doing or repairing, damn it, he did it. Ultimately it was the final months of not being able to contribute around the house that broke him.

None of Joe's practical household mechanical skills or fix-it prowess rubbed off on his ten-thumbed, book-writing twin sons. We could barely decipher the proper end of an electric skill saw let alone install a variable speed ceiling fan. Yet during our years spent in the music business, plus another decade-plus writing books, Joe had become our biggest fan and closest confidant. He'd encouraged us to continue in the tough writing game.

He wanted to know what biography projects we had in mind to develop. At the time, we were researching a complicated and ambitious modern-day story involving the Chicago mob. Joe told us about the time in East Pittsburgh in 1960 when he and his brother Emil would do floor covering jobs for a wealthy wise guy who ran the local numbers racket. The man had offered to invest in their little shop in exchange for them helping to cover his tracks on the money-laundering operation with a secure back room. Joe declined.

Despite the arguing and vitriol of the 1960s and 1970s between father and sons, we'd made our peace. It was through Joe that we'd realized the importance of "giving back," and that the process didn't necessarily equate itself with spirituality or religion.

That's why Joe took an avid interest in our San Quentin writing class. Whether or not we were fulfilling the dream that he didn't realize didn't matter—the mention of a capacity Friday night crowd in the H-Unit classroom pleased him immensely. Each week, once we cleared the front East gate and were on our way across the bridge back home, we'd phone up Joe, who was always curious as to what subject had been written about that week.

Every few months, we would bundle the finer class assignments and e-mail him the best of the men's latest writings. One short

325-word piece was written by Steve Ramone, our parole-jumping, 300-pound, tattooed ex-student.

Ramone's piece was culled from a writing assignment we'd dished out called "A Rare Moment of Spiritual Tranquility." The assignment was the result of a sudden change of plans during one class after challenging the men to write some highly charged, emotional Dennis-Miller-styled negative rants. While the rants were forceful and at times hilarious during the ReadBack, we could feel the temperature and temperament of the room rise to an uncomfortable level. So we decided to tone things down and, in essence, talk the inmates down from the ledge of hostility and hysteria that we ourselves had helped instigate. Our goal was to divert them towards a more peaceful and tranquil state of spirituality, be it religious or whatever.

Turned out, our little plan worked. The more tranquil assignment took us from anger and frustration to vivid descriptions of exotic places like Key West, or a Harley-Davidson journey snaking down Highway 1 along the rugged California coast to Hearst Castle. The writing turned inward and introspective. One writer summoned God through an acid trip, and the inmates' characterization of spirituality and tranquility was wide-ranging.

Yet Ramone's short piece was the one that affected us most considerably, as it did Joe. In a few hundred words, Ramone described his daily trek from H-Unit up the hill to North Block, to his job as a clerk dispensing canteen items and other necessities to impatient inmate customers. It was a job he detested. During Ramone's daily stroll to and from H-Unit, he had found a small square-foot parcel of land that, if he stood on it perfectly, revealed an awe-inspiring Marin County panorama. The contrast between the magnificent view that he'd discovered and the ominous surrounding walls and gun towers that Ramone witnessed standing on this precise spot moved him to put pen to paper.

We sent Ramone's piece to Joe, and once he read it, he printed a copy, folded it in half, and stashed it in his Bible to share with the members of his church congregation as an example of the kind of prose we were coaxing out of so-called rowdy criminals. While Joe was a regular churchgoer, he was not of the overzealous or fundamentalist variety, unlike some of his evangelical peers. He was a simple, commonsense guy, not bound by strict or unyielding doctrine. In other words, like Johnny Cash, Joe walked it rather than talked it, which is why the simplicity of Ramone's mystical moment touched his heart.

The morning of Joe's massive stroke, my mother handed the phone over to a firefighter who had answered her emergency 911 distress call. Things didn't sound good, so we jumped into the car, driving the sixty-five miles to get to Joe's bedside. A week later, on February 9, 2009, Joe made his exit from the material world, taking care not to linger too long and bring undue hardship to his immediate family, who tended to him until he died. He was 84.

Joe's memorial service drew a few hundred admirers at his neighborhood church, located two or three miles down the road from his home. While the church's pastor presided over the religious aspects of the ceremony, we set out to balance things by offering our off-the-cuff anecdotal remembrances. One former neighbor recalled Joe's loyalty, and how he'd stood up for him when he and his partner became the first gay couple on the block. What followed was a very close and meaningful friendship between them and our mother and father. His speech revealed what made Joe so special, and it proved to be a tough act to follow when it came time for us to speak.

As Kent took the mic, he cleared his throat, wondering if he could make it through his short prepared speech in one emotional piece. After a few short personal reminiscences, he delivered his final words.

"You can tell a lot about a person by what they find beautiful and artistic," he told the crowd. "In Joe's case, I'd like to read a short passage, something that he found inspiring. Strangely enough, this isn't a Bible verse, nor is it something composed by a great prophet or religious scholar. Rather, it was scribbled in a few minutes by a 300-pound, tattooed convict jailed for jumping parole on a carjacking and robbery charge. It's called 'The Long Walk.'"

Pulling out a folded sheet of paper from his back pocket, Kent laid Ramone's writing out on the pastor's pulpit and then laid it on the crowd, reading the short piece in its entirety, just as he had at Bobby Lee's memorial.

The Long Walk

I leave work late; my feet hit the pavement hard as my co-workers head off to H-Unit ahead of me.

The Lower Yard is closed.

The Gym has started rolling the Orange* off to chow, but they are a separate entity, their own circle of greed, hustle, and chatter. They pass by and I am alone.

From the top steps of the Upper Yard, I can see far, the bay and the hills beyond teem with other people's lives and the cluster of traffic. I breathe it all in and for a few moments I am taken away from this place.

Down, I take the steps, one by one.

Not fast, but slow, easy. Not in a hurry, as the view disappears and the concrete walls close back in around me.

The yard is empty. The gunners hidden in their towers, as now, the only thing that exists is the pavement between me and the walls of H-Unit.

How long is the walk?

A half mile. A quarter mile. Maybe just a few hundred feet. I don't know. The temptation to count the steps is there inside me, but I feel that it will destroy this magical moment for me.

You see, in a place filled with five thousand voices, this is the only place I am alone.

Between the Upper Yard and H-Unit, in the space of a day when all convicts are called on to be filed, counted, and put away for the night, walking next to the baseball field and smelling the grass, watching the seagulls circle and the ducks find home on the green field, all those voices, all those souls now fade away.

This is peace, a small oasis of paradise in a day full of drama, dreams, and pain.

It is here, in this long walk that I am truly alone, at peace, and I smile at the sun and slow my step.

I am in no hurry.

---

* The "Orange" refers to incoming convicts who are housed in "reception," which was located in West Block at the time this piece was written. The men are given medical tests and are then classified, assigned, and shipped off to an "appropriate" California state institution.

CHAPTER 20

Strange Justice

These Are a Few of My Favorite Things . . . adrenaline rushing, a bank robbery, a jewelry store heist, a high-speed chase, escaping the cops where your heart hammers so hard you can see it outside your chest. Driving off-road, airborne over ditches, trees, the smell of pine saplings torn by the getaway car, burning, heating against a red hot exhaust. Driving fast, racing, skiing, wilderness mountains, a mountain stream, riding a bike, and a cold drink of water from the stream. Spontaneous road trip. Gone.

—David Martin, from *Yard Time, Hard Time, Our Time* 7-18-08

At the risk of digressing from our story, we need to explore the basics of crime and punishment. Sentencing and doing time. Release and parole. Rehabilitation. What does it mean in practical terms? Let's examine an everyday life. How does the "average" convict end up in prison? How do they get caught up in California's 67 percent revolving door recidivism rate? How do these convicts enter a convoluted justice system?

Take the case of one ex-inmate student: David Martin. His story gives us valuable insight as to how an average felon (if there is such a thing) actually ends up in prison, and in David's case, how charges can escalate, resulting in more and more time spent inside.

First, let's be honest. We can't be 100 percent objective. For starters, we don't have access to his court transcripts. Nor input from the prosecution, defense, victims, or family members. Yet if David Martin's story is even 50 percent truth, it's hard not to find it engrossing. In the grand argument over law and order and crime and punishment, let's focus on the particulars of one offender instead of dealing with abstractions, statistics, and absolutes.

"David Martin" was raised in the San Francisco Bay Area and grew up in a bohemian family environment. His father worked for one of the premier San Francisco rock 'n' roll bands of the 1960s.

"My dad was an anti-authority hippie," David recalled. "When I was in high school doing drugs, mostly pot and cocaine, one day my mother pointed over at San Quentin and said to me, 'Keep it up, David, and you'll end up over there.'"

And unfortunately, David's mother had deftly predicted his fate. In the mid-eighties, young David—out of control, out of school, and out of work—defiantly robbed a bank.

"It was Friday, October 23, 1985," he began. "I walked into one of those Asian money banks where it was rare to see a round eye. I purposely chose that type of bank, knowing that eyewitnesses would likely say something like 'all white guys look alike.'"

After the robbery, David fled the Bay Area for Atlanta. What he didn't count on was that his FBI wanted poster would cross the desk of a major crimes task force lieutenant—who happened to also be a longtime friend of David's family and who worked for the San Francisco PD. Five months later he was apprehended in Tampa/St. Pete while attempting to flee the country. David ended up in a federal prison in Talladega, Alabama.

"My first time in the joint and my ass ends up in 'Bama!'"

Starting in Alabama, David worked his way through the federal system with stops at Federal Correction Institution (FCI) El Reno, FCI Terminal Island in Southern California, and ultimately, FCI Phoenix. David was released early from FCI Phoenix in September 1989 after doing just short of two thirds of his six-year bank robbery sentence. He was released a couple of months early because he had rescued a prison contract worker who'd been accidentally electrocuted in FCI Terminal Island.

The bank robbery conviction left him scarred: a federal offender mark and a dark cloud would follow him the rest of his life. After being released from federal prison, in the process of putting his life back together, David became an electrician and went to work for a company his father had founded in 1971.

During the late nineties, while going through drug treatment, David shoplifted a store in Chico, California. While being chased by store security, David ran from the scene but was caught. Using this as a wake-up call, and wanting to avoid doing jail time for the shoplifting, David and his wife fled from their drug environment and opted for a fresh start by absconding to the Great Northwest.

"I became David Martin because the Seattle phone book had about a hundred guys with that same name. Since I didn't want to steal anyone's identity, I simply made one up."

With his wife pregnant with their first child, David got a job as a mining superintendent, part of a $25 million dollar engineering project in Montana. Once the baby arrived, David worked long hours, six days a week, pulling a solid salary. As the months passed, it looked as if David's Chico shoplifting charge might remain lost in the pre-9/11 bureaucratic paper shuffle.

"I was pulled over once. When they tried running my name and social security number through their computers, they couldn't find me. I insisted, saying, 'I've got to be in there,' so I gave them my journeyman's ID from work. Scratching their heads, they let me go. Cops in Montana hated computers anyway."

After a year in Montana, David was turned in as the result of an anonymous tip. California came calling with an outstanding arrest warrant for the shoplifting charge in Chico. By the time David was arrested, the charge had been escalated to armed robbery by the Butte County District Attorney.

"Somehow the DA got the ex-Marine Special Forces guy who was working as a security guard for the store to say that he was afraid of me. Even though I was an unarmed dope fiend running away from him, they claimed that his fear constituted armed robbery."

What originally carried a maximum of six months in county jail was being filed under the California Three Strikes Law, carrying a minimum of 25 years to life! The day his trial began, the DA offered David a deal of 18 years, which he turned down. The trial ended in a hung jury, and consequently the DA's next offer shrunk to five years.

"Everybody told me to take the five years, including my lawyer. With a [previous] hung jury, I thought I had leverage, except I had no money left to rehire my attorney. So I took on a public defender and decided to fight. When we got to the day to pick a jury, the DA came up with a new offer of three years. Since I'd fought the case the past year from jail, I only had three or four months of time left to do. So I took the three years. Unfortunately this came with a trumped up armed robbery conviction."

David's next stop was reception at Tracy State Prison, where he was processed into the California Department of Corrections system. He asked to be sent to San Quentin or the nearby medical unit in Vacaville. At the time, as a result of tumors growing in his throat, David could barely talk. In jail, his nickname became Whispers. When it came time to be reassigned, David was sent to Susanville, California.

"At that point, I couldn't talk, I could barely whisper. Inside Susanville, I got a job as a porter in the gym, except the officer in charge fired me because he couldn't hear what I was saying. Every time I tried to get medical attention for my throat, the doctors claimed I was bucking for elective surgery. Like breathing and talking is elective?

"By then I felt like a hostage. I couldn't talk. I couldn't call my family to tell them where I was. So I filed a grievance citing cruel, inhumane, and unusual punishment. Within two months, they shipped me to Vacaville."

Vacaville was where David hit the law books.

"I studied my transcripts until I realized that the judge sentenced me illegally." When David was sentenced, along with time served, the judge applied 15 percent earned credits, also known as "good time." In reality, David was eligible for half-time, a 50 percent credit earning.

"After filing in court, I was told my motion had been granted, and I was to be released. By then, I was already 88 days late from my original release date, and suddenly I was on parole."

Once on parole, David was ordered to return to where he had been apprehended and not his current residence. Instead of San Francisco (where his wife and child now were), he was sent back to Chico, where he'd had the prior arrest for shoplifting. (Note: This is quite common. California prison inmates are often paroled back to the place where they were arrested as opposed to where they might have family or access to support programs or employment.)

"Suddenly I'm a resident in Butte County, but I didn't know anybody in Chico. So I went to the closest California state campground I could find near Chico and rented a campsite on a monthly basis. When my parole officer asked for proof of where I was living, I handed him the receipt from the campground. Site #22, Lake Oroville. I was living in a tent!"

But then David started using drugs again. After the police found drugs on him, he was sent directly to San Quentin as a parole violator for seven months. While serving his time in H-Unit, David was having throat problems, exacerbated in part by a cloud of secondhand cigarette smoke he breathed 24/7 inside the reception quarters, where newly arrived inmates are processed. To qualify for surgery to fix his throat, David filed an avalanche of 602's, the state prison system's standard grievance form.

"My throat bled. I couldn't talk. I needed clean air and medical attention. While I was at work, somebody went through my locker and revealed my legal work and complaint paperwork to the white shot-caller on the yard. He said something like, 'This guy is going to get tobacco banned from the prison system. He's your enemy because he's stirring up all kinds of shit.'"

"When I got back from work that day," David recalled, "I had to fight four white dudes because they thought that I would be responsible for any impending ban on smoking. I ended up in the infirmary, after which they sent me to the Carson section of San Quentin, a.k.a. the Hole. I was doing seven months, a 210-day violation for possession of drugs. I did 215 days, most of it in the Hole." Angry beyond words for being held past his release date with no explanation, upon his release David went underground.

"Once I got out, I played right into their hands. I didn't want to see another cop again, so I ran, jumped parole, knowing that one day I would get caught."

While on the lam, on December 17, 2002, David walked into a hardware store in San Rafael.

"I walked in ready to boost a tool. Maybe I wanted to get caught, who knows? I looked up at the video camera and smiled, sticking the tool under my shirt. Except suddenly I got a bad feeling that what I was about to do was wrong. So I put the tool back on the shelf and walked out of the store. Four guys followed me and put me under citizen's arrest."

Once the San Rafael Police arrived, they joked about the croak of David's voice. The officers at the station escalated his charge of "shoplifting" to second degree burglary and assault.

"Except I hadn't stolen anything, nor did I assault anybody."

With his past as a bank robber, the Chico shoplifting (armed robbery) conviction, and his current charge, David was to be tried as a three-strike offender. David would face 25-years-to-life if convicted.

"The public defender brought me what he considered a great deal—an offer of eight years, four months. Since I planned to fight anyway, I turned the deal down. So they yanked the deal off the table, and I was back to facing 25-to-life for shoplifting. In other words, three strikes and I'm gone."

During the trial, the foreman asked to speak to the judge. Some jurors, including the foreman, were concerned that the case might be a three-strike case. The group of jurors wanted no part in this brand of "strange justice."

"Ladies and gentlemen," the judge addressed the jury, "sentencing is my job. You are only here to determine innocence or guilt."

David Martin was quickly found guilty and, as prophesied by his mother years ago, he would wind up in San Quentin again, to serve 25 to life for intent to shoplift. His conviction was for second-degree burglary.

But David caught a legal break in the form of a "Romero Motion." If a prior strike has happened a long time ago or if the prior strike is less serious, a defendant can file a Romero Motion to escape being sentenced under California's tougher Three Strikes Law. As a result, the judge sentenced him to seven years under the rules of two strikes.

"I guess eighty percent of seven years was better than 25-to-life."

The Year It All Went Wrong

(Based on and inspired by the song by Michael McDermott)

The Year It All Went Wrong. Nye, Montana. It was a bad year, the year it all went wrong. It started out as the best of years, it was the year 2000, and I was on top of the world. A long-term job, financial security, a wife, new baby. I had it all, including a warrant out of sunny California for armed robbery. Wow. That ruined my year. Minding my own business, living out in the lost and lonely country of Montana and a damn pesky warrant pops up. The cold steel of the handcuffs on a snowy day bit hard into my wrists. I'm marched in and out of courtrooms from Billings to Big Timber with magistrates shaking their fists. Somewhere above the clouds in Montana, I fell down. I fell from the top of the world, from a mountain castle. I fell into the sticky tentacles of an insatiable beast, the California Dept. of Corrections. It's the year every last cent I knew turned on me and ran. Freedom flew from my grasp and I landed in the can. My dog ran away and the sad cat's bowl sat empty that year. My life's in the skids, the year it all went wrong.

—David Martin, from Yard Time, Hard Time, Our Time 3-6-09

When David first turned up in our writing class in 2008, he resisted the idea of taking education classes. Bitter after his arrest, he attended his committee evaluation meeting with a chip on his shoulder.

"When they told me I should be programming, I told them, hell no, I probably have more education than you. I had become a certified firefighter in SQ and a journeyman electrician on the streets. Stuff your school, I said. I was Mr. Tough Guy. So they put me on C status."

C Status meant zero privileges. No visits. No canteen. No yard. No nothing.

"So I went groveling back. I told the committee people, 'I'm sorry I blew up at you guys. I was having a bad day.'"

So David changed his tune and started programming. He became a trusted inmate tapped for clerical duties. He took on the role of an inmate leader and rights advocate in his dorm. He organized the men for clean clothes and sheets, to have them regularly laundered at least once a week, which had not been the case in nearly two years! He also noticed that H-Unit hadn't hosted a Men's Advisory Committee (MAC) meeting in over two years.

"I became a housing clerk for my dorm. We would engineer neighborhoods. The Mexican Paisas wanted to live together. So did the Sureños, blacks, American Indians, and everybody. Certain area codes, gangs, and cliques stuck together. At any given time on the H-Unit yard, there might be as many as 30 different subgroups of people who formed a 'car' [a group comprised of "like-minded or like-regional" inmates]. I was part of the San Francisco 'car' because of being born there and because they were mellow. They seldom enforced the hard yard politics. They would look the other way rather than take time to hate on someone for sharing a smoke with a black guy.

"Because I didn't smoke or use, I didn't need much money in my canteen account to get by. Hot meds were the thing to go on, but I wouldn't. A third of the yard was already on Methadone or morphine. Prison was the last place I'd want to get high in. Why bother in a place where having your wits about you at all times can save your life?"

In addition to our class, David studied yoga and completed other classes in writing and parenting. Inside H-Unit, he became an industrious and clever inmate and a prison yard wheeler-dealer.

"All the years I was on H-Unit, I ran tobacco. I had a monopoly going. I was 'prison rich.' People sought me out. I had boxes of silver jewelry I got from trading tobacco. The going price I set for a standard wedding band was six cigarettes. I could roll 80 cigarettes from a pouch that ordinarily produced 50. The most expensive cigarette I sold was $13.10 for one pinner. I could take a Marlboro and cut it in thirds and sell all three pieces for three bucks apiece."

David's tobacco sources ranged from staffers to Caltrans highway cleanup crew members. With his release pending and knowing that the $200 gate money he had coming from the state wouldn't go far, to finance a nest egg David converted his tobacco revenues into postage stamps. Each day he would mail out 40 stamps (the daily legal limit an inmate was allowed to send) to a friend on the outside.

Once released, David found the outside world accelerated, transformed, and ever changing.

"I had almost $4,000 in stamps saved, which I sold on eBay for 80 and 90 percent of face value. Getting out was like floating on air. Outside in the real world, everything moves so fast. Once the lights go out, it's peaceful and quiet, so quiet, my ears rang from the years of noise I'd heard. I never thought that 'quiet' could be so high-pitched and unnerving."

What most folks found routine, David found terrifying.

"I was out three days when my wife took me shopping. I got lost in IKEA. I felt trapped inside. I couldn't get out. The experience flashed me back to being locked up, and I didn't like it at all."

David's top priority was to reunite with his family.

"I had five kids from three wives. I wasn't always there for my family because I was too selfish. I wanted to fix that. Then my kids sought me out and now we spend lots of time together, especially on holidays, weekends, and a few family reunions. Even my sister, niece, and nephews visiting from Australia."

David currently works as an electrician and builder. Living modestly and drug-free, he's proud of a son who attends college. He stays in close contact with most of his family, especially his aging, ailing father. He's active with an art group called We Players ("transforming public places into realms of participatory theater") which operates, ironically, on the island of Alcatraz.

One of David's art projects was to convert an Alcatraz prison cell into an art installation. The cell is wallpapered with pages from four years of David's journals, printed by hand in tiny seven-point-font-sized lettering. He wrote so small because he didn't know where he might find enough writing paper in the Hole to serve out his sentence. By carefully calculating his release date, he apportioned his journal so that the very last available page of paper documented his final day in prison.

Using David as an example, the average cost of incarceration isn't cheap. Seven years times 12 months equal 84 months. Doing 80 percent of 84 months amounts to just over 67 months, or 5.6 years. Five point six years times the estimated annual cost of approximately $52,000 per state prison inmate comes out to $291,200. Double that amount for the multiple throat surgeries that David required, and the state spent well over half a million dollars incarcerating him. Had he been sentenced to the full 25-years-to-life as recommended by his prosecutors, after serving the required 80 percent of his sentence—20 years—he would have cost taxpayers approximately $1,040,000, not counting the medical bills for multiple throat surgeries.

Now discharged and off parole, David lives freely in Northern California. So far, he is winning the recidivism battle, determined not rejoin the 67 percent . . . except for that Alcatraz cell that he turned into an unlikely work of art.

CHAPTER 21

Are You Ready for
a Throwdown?

After five years, "Finding Your Voice on the Page" was kicking serious ass. Voices were hurtling off the page. Lots of show and a minimum of tell. H-Unit had become the literary mecca for San Quentin (at least in our eyes). The writing was crisp, which meant that 1) there was a respectable talent pool among the characters populating the wily H-Unit yard; and 2) our method of speed writing and ReadBacks was working.

Then we hit a serious lull in 2009.

We realized that at some point we would have to fight off complacency, which lurked at every corner. And these were dodgy times. The economy sucked. The state was slashing budgets and the pay and overtime for CO's was drastically cut, which made them especially testy. At times the yard would close without notice and the education programs got caught in the crossfire. In domino fashion, the relationship between inmates and guards would sour. Skirmishes and violence affected the whole institution. At one point, San Quentin was locked down for three solid weeks, with all "ed" programs cancelled. Momentum had ground to a halt. After a recent tide of inmate releases, our stable of consistent student writers had fallen below the Mendoza line of twenty students which, frankly, was cramping our style. While we wanted the men to stay on top of their writing skills, all of these factors were pushing against us.

We asked ourselves, is the class winding down? Did the curriculum need a transfusion of new ideas? There were reasons to worry. We noticed the men were getting casual, a little cocky about their writing and erratic with their attendance habits. We worried that the class had exceeded its shelf life. Were we being taken for granted? After one week when we dipped below twenty students, the shit hit the fan.

Keith checked through the recent attendance sheets and found that a few guys had been signing in their buddies in absentia who had skipped class. The official roll sheet listed twenty-seven students. There were actually only seventeen students present.

"Rolf," Keith said to the in-class clerk, "revamp the roll sheet and get rid of the quitters."

"Listen, guys," Kent said as he angrily prepared to dismiss class for the night. "We need to adhere to more stringent attendance regulations. Three no-shows and you're out. These are rules we didn't need to enforce before. Believe it or not, we have standards to adhere to."

We shook our heads as class ended. We were in a lousy mood. It had been a rough week. A possible sweet book gig had fallen through, and we were shaking off the initial throes of disappointment after the potentially hot client had gotten cold feet and suddenly flaked out, though his manager was gung ho about him doing a memoir.

We had already asked ourselves on the drive over, should we put the class on ice and risk eradicating the momentum that had taken us years to build? Or should we kill it off for good with a decent finish? Having Friday nights off didn't sound like such a bad idea.

Willie W. walked up, sensing our disgust. He had been a four-year veteran of the class and over the past two years we'd watched his beard grow longer, like a character you'd see starring in *Masterpiece Theatre*. Willie had had his ups and downs doing his time. The class helped him persevere from Friday to Friday.

"I know you guys are pissed off and I don't blame you," Willie said, "but I just want to let you know how much we appreciate your coming in. These last few years have been real dark for me. I wasn't doing my time very well at the beginning, but being in your class helped get me through this and I wanna thank you for that."

As the rest of the students filed out, heads down, tablets and folders in hand, we looked at each other and agreed, what we needed was a bump, a jolt, a big event to shake things up for these guys. But what?

We found our answer on, of all things, the Food Network on cable TV.

The Food Network is unavailable inside the walls of Q, and it's a damned good thing. Watching sumptuous close-ups of freshly baked cupcakes and desserts, sizzling steaks and barbecue, and meticulously arranged gourmet meals would be torture to anyone with a decent palate beyond KFC who was locked up. Over the past few years, we'd become fans of New York City restaurateur Bobby Flay, the network's most visible superstar and Iron Chef.

Throwdown with Bobby Flay, his highly rated show on the network, has a simple premise. Bobby finds out who makes the best mac 'n' cheese, crab cakes, meatloaf, jerk chicken, or other standard favorite. Then, hiding behind the ruse of filming a Food Network special featuring these experts and their specialty dishes, he emerges mid-show to challenge them: "Are you ready for a Throwdown?"

Flay then prepares *his* adaptation of *their* signature dish, serving up both his and theirs to a roomful of fans. Then two esteemed judges step out of the shadows to select a winner. The show's concept is brilliant and entertaining. Bobby usually gets his culinary ass handed to him, but occasionally he stuns the audience and the experts by pulling out a victory.

"What if we held a Literary Throwdown?" Kent asked Keith.

Originally, our plan called for bringing in a group of creative writing MFA graduate students from a nearby art college to do a cooperative writing assignment with the class. During the week we would type up the results and on the following Friday everyone would return (plus our three appointed judges) as we read aloud the grad students' writings versus an equal number of our students' writing. The panel of judges would then determine the winning team.

Keith, the more cautious and skeptical, shook his head.

"No way. First off, we'll get creamed. Second, some of our best writers are gone, and we need to rebuild the team. Third, it'll be an insurmountable bureaucratic nightmare getting this thing okayed and signed off. Fourth, it'll destroy the confidence of the men."

"But what if we win?" Kent countered.

"No way," Keith barked back. "C'mon, it's a stupid idea."

"I say we put it to the men. Let them decide."

The following Friday, we brought it up to the class.

"Are you ready for a Throwdown?" Kent asked the guys, pointing his finger at them and imitating Flay. He was met with crooked stares.

We explained the idea of a Literary Throwdown. And thanks to our lit agent's last minute suggestion, we raised the bar of the competition significantly higher by offering to bring in actual *published authors* instead of seasoned college grads.

Kent explained the challenge and the concept. "What if we bring in a group of published authors and you guys take them on in a writing competition held right here in the classroom? We'll call it The San Quentin Literary Throwdown." Kent continued his pitch, "Keith thinks it's a very bad idea. I say, let's do it. What do you guys think?"

The responses varied around the room. Frenchie, a black former SoCal drug kingpin, whose opinion we respected the most, sat stoic and quiet, rubbing his chin in contemplation. Raul, sitting up front, gave the idea a thumbs-up. Tim, one of the white elder statesmen in the class, was poker-faced. He was cynical and had his doubts.

"They won't let you guys do it."

"They," meaning the warden's office, and the custody staff from the third shift. Prison is an environment built upon routine to which both the CO's and the men adapt and adhere. Maybe Keith was right. This was already starting to sound like one huge bureaucratic pain in the ass. Then a young bald-headed cranium-tattooed Mexican named Arturo seated in the back raised his hand.

"You guys actually think we have an ice cube's chance in hell of winning?"

"Yeah, sure, why not?" Kent shrugged optimistically. There were two distinct camps in the room: the confident and cocky (like Kent) and the skeptical (like Keith). Then Big H, one of the outspoken black "OG" writers, brought up his primary concern.

"Will there be women writers in the room? And if so, and we do this thing, can we conduct ourselves appropriately without acting the fool?"

Big H had a valid point. But the bigger question remained, were the men ready, willing, and able to compete?

"This entails putting you guys through a rigorous six-week training program," Keith offered. "We need to get you back in shape for some stiff competition. It's like athletes—you'd be working out for the play-offs."

Kent grabbed a red marker and began scribbling on the whiteboard.

"Let's analyze the situation by writing down the advantages and disadvantages. Call 'em out."

Advantage: Guys in prison have more life experience and more colorful stories.

Disadvantage: Authors have college degrees and loads more education.

Advantage: We'd be writing on our turf with home field advantage.

Disadvantage: They've been writing longer than us, possibly most of their lives.

Advantage: The published writers might not be used to writing off the cuff and in longhand.

Disadvantage: The published writers are very well-read.

We went around the room to gauge response. Andre, a black hip-hopper writing his own cookbook, said yes. Dexter, a twenty-something Native American, gave us a taciturn but adamant thumbs-down. Willie, whose writing skills we'd watched blossom over the past two years, nodded his head affirmatively. JFK, the bearded, long-haired, homeless-looking Deadhead, was in. Even our weakest link, Hawkins, a slim, black, learning impaired "J-cat" and former crackhead, was in.

Frenchie, the last person in the class to vote, broke his silence. "I'll tell you what: If you guys come up with a super cool writing topic, and we can keep it real, then we'll win this thing for you."

Frenchie's belated response lit the fuse. The enthusiasm in the room shot up. The Throwdown was on.

Kent, in a moment of irrational exuberance, made a reckless promise. "I'll tell you what: If we do this, I'm gonna pull some favors and get three Hollywood screenwriters to be the judges."

Keith gave Kent the stank eye. "Terrific. Look what you've gotten us into, bro. Now we have to find six hot published writers willing to write inside a freaking prison *and* three Hollywood screenwriters to fly up and judge."

Plus, life hadn't exactly been hunky dory in H-Unit lately.

There had been fights and lockdowns, principally among the Vallejo blacks and "CoCo County" whites and, once again, the Norteños versus everybody. A couple of students, Danny and Bullhorn, had recently been relegated to the Hole for jumping into the middle of the fray. Plus, the inmate "head counts" had been consistently running late, delaying our class for up to an hour until everyone was fed, inmates counted, and all kitchen cutleries accounted for. (A week prior, a meat thermometer had gone missing.) We needed two Fridays clear of lockdowns, delays, gang incidents, and swine flu quarantines, otherwise a Throwdown just wasn't going to fly. In other words, we needed a logistical miracle.

Keith rummaged through his class folder and found a piece of paper from the lesson bag and wrote something on the whiteboard.

> Just write. Get a flow going. See what you got in you. Be creative. It's called creative writing, right? Put some words on the page and let the pen do the work. Let the words take you away to another place or another time.

"Who wrote that?" asked a nineteen-year-old skinhead named J.D. sitting by the door.

It was Colm's original mission statement from our very first class . . . back when we only had five guys in the class.

"Just a little something a guy wrote in this class a long, long time ago," Keith said, half nostalgically. "He's probably driving a truck somewhere in Brooklyn now."

CHAPTER 22

Acronyms and Throwdowns

Stuck to the window of the visitors' area was a piece of paper advertising a weekly inmate encounter group: IMPACT. IMPACT stood for "Incarcerated Men Putting Away Childish Things!" Prison programs have a way of creating amusing didactic acronyms for its homegrown groups. Then one day we received a memo that our San Quentin H-Unit program would cease to exist under its present moniker. The Success Program had morphed into . . . the "STAND UP Program." STAND UP was an equally nebulous acronym for "Successful Transitions And New Directions Utilizing Partnerships." It was probably thought up by the same bunch who acronymized IMPACT.

By March 2010 we'd celebrated the seventh anniversary of the class over drinks with our friends Jack Boulware and Jane Ganahl, the co-founders and co-directors of Litquake. Litquake—not an acronym, thank goodness—is a street-smart nonprofit cultural foundation founded in 1999 that celebrates the literary scene in the San Francisco Bay Area, as well as other areas of the country like New York City, Austin, and beyond. Each October they host the ambitious Litquake Literary Festival in San Francisco, held in a sprawling network of various venues (ranging from bookstores, nightclubs, and pubs to boutiques, coffeehouses, and Laundromats) for a weeklong series of literary events like book signings, readings, media soirées, and panel discussions. Since the Litquake Festival features hundreds of authors each year (including us), we met with Jack and Jane to discuss the ramifications of them helping us stage our very first San Quentin Literary Throwdown. Our hope was that they could give us the names, e-mails, and contact information of some published authors who might be interested in competing against our amateur inmate writers.

Jack and Jane were intrigued with our unique contest and threw Litquake's weight behind our modest proposal. They saw the Throwdown as an opportunity for veteran authors to test their improvisational writing skills in a unique setting—behind the walls of the legendary San Quentin.

First, we composed an invitation letter detailing the Throwdown concept. We explained that we were looking for six distinguished authors to set aside two Friday nights to participate in a writing contest.

The first Friday session would be spent writing on an impromptu topic for forty minutes, followed by an informative discussion between the writers and inmates on the art of writing and publishing.

The second Friday, we would read aloud to the class six writing entries from the published authors and six entries chosen from our cadre of inmates, and the audience for that session would include a three-person panel of judges. The twelve pieces would be randomly sequenced without bylines. After the judges awarded points for each piece, the scores would then be tallied and totaled and the winning team would be announced at the end of class! Who would prevail? The seasoned published authors, or our gang of renegade amateurs?

Litquake e-mailed our invite to cutting-edge authors in the Bay Area. We were looking for six brave men and women to join us for two Fridays of rapacious literary competition. Was it a tall order to request such a writer to submit him or herself to such a daunting experience?

Turned out, probably not, as we filled up our six-author dance card in less than a week—three of them responded within an hour. One interested writer had to bow out after his wife disapproved, but when the smoke cleared, we had chosen six published authors specializing in a variety of genres. Columnist and author Alan Black had just published an arcane satire entitled *Kick the Balls: A Bruising Season in the Life of a Suburban Soccer Coach.* (As mentioned earlier, Black was the general manager at the Edinburgh Castle public house, which had hosted the class's only broadcast reading back in 2003.) Joining Black was David Corbett, an edgy crime fiction author of four acclaimed thrillers with such wicked titles as *Blood of Paradise, The Devil's Redhead, Done for a Dime,* and *Do They Know I'm Running?* Ex-convicted bank robber and journalist Joe Loya, who wrote *The Man Who Outgrew His Prison Cell,* volunteered to return behind bars as a civilian. Novelist Anne Marino, who penned a dark, sensual tome called *The Collapsible World,* was the only female of the group, and Bucky Sinister, an adroit humorist and savvy street corner poet, also signed on. Sinister specialized in books dealing with recovery and addiction, with freaky titles like *All Blacked Out Nowhere To Go* and *Get Up: A 12-Step Guide to Recovery for Misfits, Freaks, and Weirdos.* Rounding out our six-author lineup was Litquake's Jack Boulware. Turns out Jack, who had just published an outstanding oral history of American punk rock called *Gimme Something Better,* couldn't resist joining our madcap Throwdown escapade.

Suddenly we were in business! Not only was our esteemed group of writers generously willing to give us two Fridays of their time, but they had to submit to being cleared by the state of California to gain access into the prison. Asking for confidential birthdates, driver's license numbers, and proper full names (mildly tricky for a gang of scribes, some of whom write under pen names) proved to be a little awkward. And how embarrassing would it have been if, for some cryptic reason, one of our talented wordsmiths was actually turned down access to visit a state penitentiary?

With a quality stable of authors nailed down, it was time to deliver on our end, to provide the contest with an esteemed trio of Hollywood screenwriters to serve as judges. Our first phone call went out to a close friend who is both a novelist and a screenwriter. Michael Tolkin is well-known as the novelist and screenwriter for *The Player,* the classic film directed by Robert Altman and starring Tim Robbins. When we contacted Michael, one of the most gifted writers we know, he had just finished the script for the movie *Nine,* starring Daniel Day-Lewis.

To round out our trio of judges, we reached out to a pair of eccentric but zany identical twin brothers named Logan and Noah Miller. They had just written and directed their first excellent feature film, called *Touching Home,* which starred Ed Harris. The Miller twins had penned *Either You're in or You're in the Way,* perhaps the only narrative nonfiction book (besides this one) written by identical twins and told in the unique style of "dual-first-person." Originally hailing from Marin County, the Millers heartily accepted our offer to judge the proceedings during week number two.

Voilà! The First Annual San Quentin Literary Throwdown was set and scheduled to take place on June 10 and 18, 2010.

"Well, guys, it's a done deal," Kent said to the guys, pumping his fist. *"The shit is on!"* We grinned proudly at our denim-clad pupils. Once again we had miraculously come through on our promises— Hollywood screenwriters and all. We were excited as hell to deliver the news.

Suddenly the room went uncharacteristically mum for a few seconds. As we read through the list of the six opponents and their body of work, the vibe became tense. Tim P., one of our best writers—and the most cynical guy in the room at any given time—nodded his head incredulously. Nobody had thought we'd actually come through. Now the men were committed to compete under some pretty tough constraints: forty minutes of impromptu writing—first takes, with little or no rewrites. Our only hope was that our nifty crop of literati was as addicted to their laptops as they were to their BlackBerries and iPhones. Our best chance of victory would be through the old school use of pen and paper.

Surveying the classroom, more than a few wondered what might happen. Would the published authors annihilate the inmates? After suffering an agonizing defeat, would the men feel they'd let us down, or worse, that they'd let *themselves* down?

Another Tim, Tim D., put up his hand. "What's the writing subject going to be?"

"Can't tell you that," Kent said. "But I will say this: it's a subject we haven't assigned before. Keith thought up the topic, and it's a good one." With only a couple classes left to train, we quickly assigned something on the lighter side, just to keep the class loose and limber. Keith passed out lyrics to a song by a singer named Garland Jeffreys called "Ballad of Me," in which the songwriter describes himself in one three-minute song. We wanted the men to do the same in a page or two in longhand.

In a matter of minutes, the room was silent as the men scribbled in their tablets. For his entry, Tim D. conjured rustic images reminiscent of *The Horse Whisperer* meets film director John Ford:

> Kicking it with my brothers out on the ranch. Faded denim, holes, with my knees sticking out, and dirty scuffed cowboy boots with dried shit on the heels. Straw hat sitting atop my blond head keeps the sun off my crew cut. Spitting in the dust. Thumbs in my pockets. Trying my darndest to be a reflection of my grizzled Pops as he broke one of our spirited mares. I was the kid my Pops would put on the mares because I was light enough to fill in for the eventual saddle that would be placed on her back . . . that is, once she got used to me.

On June 10, 2010, we met the six competing authors—Anne, Joe, Jack, David, Alan, and Bucky—in the parking lot next to the main San Quentin East Gate entrance. Nobody had made any wardrobe faux pas by showing up in denim, orange, blue, or khakis, although, just in case, we had a few extra dark oversized clothing items stashed in our car. Although Loya and Corbett had visited federal and state lockdowns before—Joe as a prisoner and David as a private detective interviewing witnesses—everybody seemed a bit uneasy. Truth be told, we were a bundle of nerves ourselves. We knew this was prison, and that anything could happen logistically at each turn. While everybody relied on us to remain calm and under control, we worried whether there would be any last-minute snafus to derail the proceedings. What if the final count or chow were delayed? What if there was a last-minute emergency lockdown or riot? Anything could happen.

We were greeted at the gate by Laura Bowman-Salzsieder, San Quentin's CPM—an acronym for Community Partnerships Manager—one of the persons responsible for (among other things) the education programs running smoothly on the inside. We introduced Laura to our motley crew of literary misfits, and took our rightful place in line waiting for gate clearance among the usual cadre of Happy Catholics armed with their guitar cases and holy books. We were not on a pious mission of mercy, nor were we there to supply spiritual sustenance. We had some Throwdown ass to kick, hoping to buck the odds and achieve victory through some stunning upset.

To our relief, everybody's name, rank, and serial number passed muster through the gate's computer system and all were given clearance to enter San Quentin's inner sanctum. Next we jumped into two vehicles and headed down the twisted miracle mile towards the H-Unit parking lot. We pointed out to our solemn guests the notorious multistoried stone edifice that was Death Row, and the raggedy Reception area where newly transferred prisoners were booked and processed. One could see the reception population in the distance dressed in their bright orange jumpsuits.

As was our custom, we waved at the gun tower as we scooted our entourage between the two remote-control closing double doors of the H-Unit entrance. Next we shepherded our guests through the frisky metal detector. After the final sign-ins, Laura huddled our apprehensive guests into the sally port area before embarking onto the dusty H-Unit yard.

Surveying the wary expressions of the writers, we thought of our own first-time anxieties going behind the walls. Laura gave us the legal rundown, warning everyone that in the event of a serious inmate uprising, correctional officers would not be legally obligated to negotiate for the release of hostages. She advised our guests not to accept any written communication or contraband items from anyone. She also reminded us that it's best to walk, not run, inside a prison yard.

As we buzzed ourselves through the last metal gate, we were followed and filmed by a crew from San Quentin TV who stalked our party as we ambled down the yard towards the front door of the classroom. We were then met at the door by our STAND UP protectorate, Jill Brown, and San Quentin's media representative, Sam Robinson, who introduced us to Nancy Mullane, a reporter from NPR (acronym for National Public Radio) assigned to cover the Throwdown for NPR's popular national *Weekend Edition* broadcast. To our surprise, Nancy pulled out a digital camera and snapped a few shots of our lit crew. We were a little taken aback, only because it was the first time in seven years that anyone had taken a photograph inside our San Quentin classroom.

Upon arrival, we handed the officer in charge a roster with the names of the almost 40 class members who would be part of the evening's festivities. Although the yard was deemed closed that night for the general population, the final count and evening chow had already cleared. We breathed a deep sigh of relief. It was 6:30 and we were right on schedule: time to announce the class over the loud-speakers and get this thing going.

The Throwdown was on! Kent advised each of the writers to grab a chair and scatter themselves around the room, so as to avoid an "us and them" vibe. As the class was announced over the loudspeakers, Keith stood out in front of the door and watched as each class member ambled towards the Education Classroom, note-books in hand. The writers later remarked how relaxed the inmates seemed. Rolf, Willie W., Tim D., Tim P., a guy whose real name was Buckshot, Eddie, Big H the OG, Dead Head Joe, JFK, JD, Frenchie, Raul, Arturo, and others filed in, nodding respectfully to the writers as they grabbed the remaining chairs. Each inmate did seem surpris-ingly loose. Maybe they were hiding their nerves just as we were. As the room filled up, we noticed we were missing one of our A-listers.

"C-Rock, where the hell is Dinero D?" we asked.

"Dunno, man. He was chillin' on his bunk last I saw," C-Rock replied.

"Jesus Christ! Go back and get him. We have a Throwdown to win."

Minutes later, with little time to spare, C-Rock returned from across the yard with Dinero, who was wearing dreadlocks and look-ing like baseball slugger Manny Ramirez. C-Rock rolled his eyes. Dinero D the Dynamic "P" had his headset on, so he'd missed the announcement.

"Damn it, Dinero, you knucklehead," Kent reprimanded him. Except he was our knucklehead, and a talent who might lead us to victory.

"Don't trip, man. I'm here," said the nonchalant Dinero D as he grabbed one of the last seats in the room.

"Remind me to moiiider you later," Keith muttered under his breath.

With the Throwdown about to commence, the room was filled to capacity. After a few minutes of humble introductions of the guest authors, a few lame jokes, and an explanation of the Throwdown rules, Keith grabbed a red marker and scrawled the long-awaited writing subject semi-legibly across the whiteboard:

DAMN! I'm Back on Square One Again!

Four dozen pairs of eyes scrutinized the seven-word phrase on the board for a minute or two. Then pens hit paper. It was like the testing scene from *Stand and Deliver*. The entire room went silent for the next forty minutes. All we could hear was the sound of scribbling on white legal pads. Once again, we flashed back to our very first class and Colm's mission statement.

> Let the pen do the work. Let the words take you away to another place or another time, anyplace at all is better than this place or worse.

Throughout the process, we heard intermittent curses, groans, and sounds of crumpling paper. A half hour later, the tension inside the room loosened as the contestants ripped out their finished sheets of paper filled with handwritten scrawl. Both writers and class members alike were relieved that the most nerve-wracking part of the competition was over. As we collected each completed piece, the result was a pile of ragged papers, each page brimming with street-smart vision and wisdom.

After leaving the prisoners behind—no hugs, only handshakes allowed—we convened to a nearby brew pub at Larkspur Landing where we tipped a few pints of black and tan with the guest authors. As our new writer friends hit their mobile devices to text and phone loved ones that they had survived their first tour of duty under razor wire and gun tower, the mood at the bar was jovial. Maybe the writers were feeling that same love/hate spell that San Quentin casts over everybody who darkens its iron doorways. As the beer flowed and the revelry continued, we felt a strange twinge of emptiness. Just over the hill, 30 of our buddies were locked down and unable to join us as we celebrated the end of Literary Throwdown Part One. On deck for next week: Part Two, the ReadBack.

During the week, we typed up nearly 40 hand-written assignments before isolating the 12 that would compete in Part Two of the Throwdown. Then it was details, details, details. Michael Tolkin made arrangements to join us at San Quentin by way of Yosemite National Park, a few hours' drive north. The Miller twins would come up from LA and meet us in Marin County. Then the phone rang again. It was Jill Brown.

"Bad news," said Jill on the other end of the line. Our hearts sunk simultaneously.

"What's up?"

"They're talking about a possible quarantine."

"Quarantine?"

"Yeah, they're concerned about this H1N1 flu virus that's going around."

"Shit, Jill. We gotta get around this somehow. We've got excited authors and screenwriters coming up from Southern Cal."

"Let me arrange a meeting tomorrow between the three of us and the assistant warden in charge of H-Unit and see if he'll give us special dispensation in case this quarantine kicks in."

"Damn," Kent said as he put down the phone. "We're screwed if this H1N1 thing kicks in. They're under no obligation to us. They can shut this thing down in a minute."

The next afternoon Jill took us to meet K.J., the assistant warden in charge of H-Unit. He was a solidly built black man who resembled a left tackle from the National Football League. K.J. had started his correctional career as a CO walking the line on North Block, where he had once caught a round of gunfire and later a knife wound on the job. Looking professionally intimidating in his smart suit and tie, K.J. was also a storefront preacher who presided over his own church congregation in nearby Richmond. That explained his charismatic side. He was known as a fair man, and we pleaded our case. We explained that we were in the midst of a unique literary competition and that the logistics of bringing in guest authors and screenwriters from near and far were staggering. It was our premiere event for our modest creative writing class. Please don't shut us down!

As we left our meeting, Jill was hopeful that an exception could be made in the event of quarantine. No guarantees were made until 24 hours before Throwdown Part Two, when the threat of quarantine was formally lifted by central command.

Whew! We had just dodged a bullet, and a rubber one at that, so to speak.

Week Two. We reserved a couple of Prison Industries-built tables for the judges, who took their seats near the back. As we greeted everyone for Part Two of the Throwdown, we explained the judging criteria. We would read all 12 entries with equal vim and vigor. Everyone in the room would be given a copy of the material to follow along with us. No bylines would be listed in the document. That way nobody would know for sure whether an inmate student or a guest author had written the entry.

Each selection would be scored on three criteria: 1) Voice: To what degree is the voice original, individual, and authentic?, 2) Clarity: How clearly is the message being conveyed?, and 3) Story: To what degree is the story unique, entertaining, and/or important? Each criterion was to be judged on a scale of one to five points, with one being poor and five being excellent.

The 12 written entries ran the gamut. Most of the prose was decidedly edgy; it wasn't altogether obvious who had written what, and the pieces covered a wide range of subject matters: a desperate man clashing with a hospital staff during the final 24 hours of his wife's life; an ex-con suffering a crippling anxiety attack after being released back into society; two hopeless, dysfunctional types meeting at a party; a pimp on the Vegas strip getting flimflammed by his own whores; a guy going crackers on his front porch brandishing a shotgun; an inmate spending the whole day trading soups and coffee for one illicit smoke that gets confiscated before he can light up; a man losing his wife to cancer and going off the rails; Mr. Family Man getting excoriated by his neighbors for having a circular lawn instead of a square one; and an ATF agent breaking down a front door and hauling a man off to jail on drug charges. By the end of each tale, the outcome was the same: Damn! I'm back at Square One again.

The ReadBack was fast-paced. To get through 12 entries, we blew through the text in just 40 minutes, roughly the same amount of time it had taken for each person to compose their entry.

Kent followed the reading with a lively discussion about the creative process with the authors, screenwriters, and inmates while Keith and Jill tallied the results in the next room. Tolkin, himself a very tough literary arts critic, stood up and told the inmates and writers that after having just read the latest 20 Under 40 issue of the *New Yorker* magazine (featuring 20 pieces by authors under 40 years of age), the prose borne from the cinder block classroom proved significantly more interesting and engaging. High praise, indeed!

After Jill and Keith totaled up the scores and rechecked the numbers a few times, they reentered the class to deliver the final results. We called the six inmates and six guest authors to the front of the room.

"The Throwdown results ended in a near dead heat," Keith announced as he wrote the point totals on the board. "Final score: 229 to 229½!" San Quentin had narrowly defeated the published authors by a mere half point!

The room surged with emotion and celebration. Grown men

wiped their eyes and six blue-clad prison brothers wore jubilant smiles. In reality, there were no losers that evening—our students, in the midst of bold competition, had successfully found their voices on the page.

Mulling over the scores later on, we saw that Judge Tolkin had given the inmates a three-point edge, 70 to 67. Noah Miller's individual scores varied but he had awarded each side an identical total of 79 points. Noah's twin brother, Logan, had given out a wide range of scores, but for Dinero D's piece about the Vegas pimp, he'd awarded a 4 ½ score instead of the full 4 or 5 points. Splitting the difference by that one-half point had become the margin by which the inmates won instead of tying.

Another bullet dodged! Instead of ending in a draw, our guys had pulled out a victory by the slimmest of margins. We were stupefied.

In the final analysis, our very first Literary Throwdown was a cliff-hanger. And while we cannot confirm this for sure, we heard that the third shift lieutenant in charge, upon hearing that the inmates had won their competition, had declared the prison yard open for everybody. Victory was sweet on the dingy H-Unit yard that night.

That Sunday we received an e-mail from our Random House editor in New York City announcing that NPR's *Weekend Edition* had broadcast the story featuring our Throwdown. People from coast to coast had heard the good news: our gang of loveable losers, the San Quentin Sweathogs, had actually won! As the late Vice President Hubert Humphrey once put it, "We were pleased as punch!"

CHAPTER 23

The Lit Crawl

After the class's first 2010 Throwdown victory, the folks at San Francisco's Litquake immediately got what we were trying to accomplish. Since its inception in 1999, we had viewed Litquake and the annual Litquake Literary Festivals as an inspiration with a similar mission to ours: exploring how to incorporate writing into the lives of everyday people. The Zimmermen axiom continued to be, "If we can write books, any damned fool can." What we coveted about Litquake was their status as a literary-based nonprofit organization, and their ability to spread their message to other cities across America. Which got us to thinking: can what works on a San Quentin prison yard work inside other institutions? Or further, could we test-run programs using prison inmates to develop literary programs and classes outside the prison walls for other underserved communities? What if we could stage a whole network of Creative Writing classes in places like old folks' homes, battered women's shelters, and halfway houses? Imagine the stories and experiences those people could write about and pass along to their families! This set us off to dream that if two guys like us could turn a classroom of prison knuckleheads into coherent writers, perhaps we could also do cool things out in the community at large. Perform a little fundraising; grow the concept little by little until we'd ventured across the state of California. Then go national, sowing the seeds of literacy while turning everyday people into prolific writers.

"Always the dreamers," Joe had said to us. Or, to quote the immortal Robert "Boogie" Sheftell, our favorite character from the 1982 movie *Diner*, portrayed by Mickey Rourke:

"If you don't have good dreams, you got nightmares."

After the Summer of 2010 Throwdown, we got a call from Litquake: Would we be interested in staging an autumn event for their upcoming Lit Crawl? Litquake's Lit Crawl, part of their enormous annual San Francisco lit festival, is an innovative event we had taken part in, one way or another, for a number of years. A Lit Crawl (as in pub crawl) goes like this: By taking over several blocks of Valencia Street—one of the hippest, artiest neighborhoods in San Francisco's Mission District—on a Saturday night, bars, cafés, bookstores, art galleries, coffee shops, and storefronts are converted into literary venues for readings, panel discussions, and media events. Litquake's challenge to us was to turn a *huge* coffee shop, Ritual Coffee Roasters on Valencia Street, into a "happening" based on our class in San Quentin. We said yes right away. The coolest part of the challenge was that once we presented our basic ideas as to what we wanted to accomplish to Jack and Jane from Litquake—that is, to portray San Quentin as our literary muse—they gave us free reign to host the entire event however we saw fit!

Now what to do? Feature the writings of the class? Bring in special guests? Host a discussion? When in doubt, we consulted the Johnny Cash Oracle. He referred us to his live *Johnny Cash at San Quentin* album.

"Tracks six and seven," we heard him utter through the oracle haze.

We latched onto a theme, our concept: "San Quentin, You've Been Living Hell to Me." It would be a combination discussion, reading, and Q&A. We would feature some material written inside the walls, and then bring up a few guests to answer questions and dispel some of the ridiculous commonly held myths about incarceration. We would track down some former students now released and have them read or share their thoughts. The title and description of our literary event was as follows:

San Quentin, You've Been Living Hell to Me

Ritual Coffee Roasters, 1026 Valencia St.

Saturday, October 9, 2010 8:30 P.M.

Many know San Quentin State Prison as a worldwide icon of crime and punishment. How many view it as a beacon of literary inspiration? Authors Keith and Kent Zimmerman take you on a "literary tour" of San Quentin State Prison through the writings done for their class, "Finding Your Voice on the Page," one of the prison's most popular weekly education classes. Inmate alumni will appear to discuss their writings and feelings about this Bay Area icon. San Quentin representatives will be on hand to discuss not only the prison's standing in the community, but the effect education and writing is having on the inmate population.

Keith and **Kent Zimmerman** write on a variety of subjects from music to crime to popular culture, and have taught writing at San Quentin State Prison for seven years.

With our concept solidified, we would stock our event with a full spectrum of relevant guests—from a former warden on down to past inmates. Our first call was to our buddy Jill Brown, the former SQ warden and STAND UP coordinator. Next, we needed a correctional officer. We called a veteran CO sergeant, Sgt. David Kilmer. Not only did he have a sterling reputation among the administration, his colleagues, and inmates, but he was a virtual historian of the infamous Q. A writer and author himself, he knew the nooks and crannies of San Quentin's checkered history. Next, we tagged Allyson West, the founder of the California Reentry Program, an organization that provides rubber-meets-the-road services for newly released H-Unit inmates.

Now we needed to recruit a few inmate alumni. Up to that point, as a general rule (with the rare exceptions previously discussed), we'd focused our work solely on the students inside and rarely kept track of students once they were released. While many departing inmates vowed to keep in touch with us upon leaving, very few had actually done so, which we understood and even agreed with, to a degree. That's because, in the final analysis, psychologically, San Quentin is a great place to leave in your rearview mirror, and we did not take that personally.

We had, however, kept in touch with a small core of former students, like Laughing Wolf, the Native American rock trivia expert. He lived not too far down the road and was officially off parole and working on his landscaping business. And there was Brian, who had been working for Goodwill Industries since being reunited with his wife and child. Brian had kept in touch with us via social networking and was making a go at his new life. We also reached out to "David Martin," who had been released two years prior and was reuniting successfully with his family and plying his trade as an electrician and builder, as well as dabbling in acting and writing.

We asked ourselves, when was the last time anyone ever held a one-hour discussion that featured a warden, a correctional officer, community servants, and former inmates, all on one tiny stage? That Saturday, the night of the Lit Crawl, we also wondered, What if nobody shows up? What if it's too scary a topic for the literary set? One hour prior to the event, we arrived at the coffeehouse in San Francisco, only to find that the joint was empty.

Damn, we're back on square one again!

Fifteen minutes before the 8:30 start time, our special guests arrived, which made us feel better. Then suddenly—bam!—the place was deluged with literati of all kinds, mostly young people. Soon every seat was taken and the adjoining counter was jammed three-deep with literary movers and shakers, including a few writers we knew and admired. By 8:28, more people were lined up and down the main wall and seated on the floor. Hallelujah! Full house!

We crammed our guest speakers onto our makeshift small stage and introduced ourselves. After a brief rap, we passed the mic around the stage. The audience was intrigued hearing the eyewitness accounts of the inner workings of San Quentin from Jill and the sergeant. Next was a strange and ironic twist: having the former inmates interact with a CO and warden who had once been their jailors. The event was yet another example of the bittersweet edifice we know as San Quentin weaving its mystical, magical spell on people. While we don't believe in the supernatural, we felt a fleeting Johnny Cash presence in the room. And then we got to thinking, Wow, Joe, our father, would have loved being here, too.

A few former inmates read their stories, and Jill spoke candidly about having to oversee a death row execution during her term. The sergeant spoke of the bygone days when H-Unit had been a tent city. Allyson talked about the realities and pressures of being released. A San Francisco boxing legend named Irish Pat Lawlor jumped up on the stage and grabbed the mic. He wowed the room by reciting a hilarious yet chilling Muhammad Ali-styled poem. While a couple of prior inmates were too shy to read their writings aloud, we happily complied and read for them. The Q&A session consisted mostly of questions posed by the younger members of the audience. "The kids," we decided, so curious and beautiful, "were all right!"

Seeing our ex-students in civilian street clothes conversing with the audience members afterwards made us realize how severe a punishment it is to be locked up and banished from society. Imagine being isolated and ostracized for a few years or months and then having to rejoin this crazy, accelerated world-in-progress. That alone might partially explain the difficulties of reentry and the unusually high recidivist rates in America. Life on the outside can seem overwhelming. Hopefully giving inmates the chance to find their voices on the page can help smooth the process.

Having received such an enthusiastic reaction from the literary general public, we couldn't wait to report to the class how it had gone down. Besides, it was time to lay not one, but two, crazy ideas on the guys back at the Q.

CHAPTER 24

Throwdown #2 and Criminal Class Review

When we started up a brand-new quarter in January 2011, we made a few wild and crazy announcements to the roomful of denim blue—a third of whom were rookies, the other two-thirds made up of seasoned veterans.

"You guys picked the best time to sign up for the class," said Kent in a tired drawl, waiting for a second wind to kick in after a long week's work.

" . . . because this year we're gonna *kick things up a notch!*"

Each STAND UP quarter has about ten Friday sessions, notwithstanding times when we're out of town and on the road seeing to our normal writing and publishing duties. The first session of each quarter is a big day for H-Unit inmates. Ordinarily we make our usual supply of utilitarian PaperMate pens and legal pads available each week, but on opening night we hand out higher quality writing utensils: the most stylish ballpoint pens we can find. For those doing time, getting a clean pad and a nice pen is no small deal.

"Kent's right," Keith concurred. "We have three new developments."

"First off," Kent jumped in, "Keith and I have a new book coming out in March." As was our custom, we would keep our students in the vocational loop during the whole process. We'd bring in preliminary cover art, copy-edit manuscripts, sample pages and fonts, and a bound copy of the uncorrected proof sent out early to critics and members of the press.

We went on to explain to the class that the new book, *Operation Family Secrets,* highlighted a major investigation of the Chicago mob by the FBI and the office of the Attorney General. We had written *Operation Family Secrets* with a principal involved in the case, Frank Calabrese, Jr. It's the story of how Frank, Jr. cooperated with the FBI to help sink the Chicago Outfit, including his father, who as a made guy had killed well over a dozen people (his specialty was a rope around the neck and a knife across the throat). It's a complicated story of family allegiances and betrayal as the book asks the question: what constitutes a white hat or a black hat character? The thought of our switching writing subjects from motorcycle clubs to mobsters and federal agents, not to mention someone who cooperated against his own father, seemed to leave a few of our students feeling unsettled. But bottom line, *Operation Family Secrets* had given us the chance to partake in some investigative journalism and to pursue an organized crime yarn.

"The publishers are setting up publicity, interviews, and book signings," added Keith. "We have a bunch of TV and radio appearances lined up in Chicago."

"And *secondly,*" Kent added, ". . . due to popular demand . . . "

A pregnant pause hung in the room. Once again we stole Bobby Flay's television line:

"Ask yourself this: Are *you* ready for a Throwdown?"

Now we had their attention.

"That's right. We've scheduled Throwdown #2 only a couple of months away. March 4th and 11th. More details forthcoming as to who your opponents will be."

Then we waited for the room to quiet down again for the third and final announcement.

"Okay, listen up!" yelled Keith over what resembled a locker-room din. "Show of hands. How many of you have had any of your writings published?"

A couple hands shyly popped up.

"Guess what?" said Kent. "This quarter, everybody in this room will have the opportunity to be published. We've just received word from a very cutting-edge literary journal in Chicago called *Criminal Class Press*."

Twice a year, the editors of this small but prestigious journal publish a couple of hundred pages of top-notch, edgy writing by various street-smart authors and writers. Some are new and unpublished; others are proven journeymen. On a few occasions, writers who appeared in *Criminal Class Press* have been discovered by editors and subsequently scored their own book deals for novels, poetry, and narrative nonfiction.

Keith jumped in. "The folks at *Criminal Class Press* have given us their next issue to be devoted 100 percent to you guys. We're calling the volume 'Yard Time, Hard Time, Our Time: The Writings of San Quentin State Prison H-Unit,' and this class will provide the content."

"Think of it!" said Kent. "They're handing us the keys to the kingdom while the lunatics take over the asylum, if you'll pardon the mixed metaphors."

Rolf raised his hand. "What exactly is this literary journal? Is it a magazine?"

"Good question," replied Keith. "This literary journal is in essence a bound trade paperback book, not a magazine. It's a paperback anthology of various writings, and you guys are driving the bus on this one. It comes out this summer."

Tim, the resident class cynic, took the floor. "This sounds great, but this place ain't gonna let you pull this off. They'll need to clear the whole process, and I don't see that happening."

We were ready for Tim P's cynicism.

"Anything can and can't happen in this place. We'll grant you that," Kent admitted. "But what if we told you we already had clearance from the administration? What if they'd already told us that as long as we secure signed releases from you as writers in this room, and no money changes hands between us and Criminal Class Press, then it's a go?"

Keith hushed the room chatter before continuing. "Guys, this is good for us. You told us about another creative writing class for the lifers that binds and publishes their writing, and gives out the copies at the end of the quarter. Well, why not find a publisher to bear the printing costs plus supply artwork for a cool cover from a nationally known artist? No money changes hands, but in return, *Criminal Class Press* will send us free books for the class. Plus it'll be available worldwide in bookstores and online so that your families and friends on the outside can buy copies of your publishing debut."

"I'll believe it when I see it," Tim cracked. The class groaned as Tim shrugged and slunk back into his chair.

"Tim," we said, "we live for the days to prove you wrong. You said that the Throwdown wasn't going to happen."

"Okay, okay," Tim relented. "Hey, I'm the lead cynic in this joint. What can I say?"

The irony of the situation was that Tim was one of our most talented and consistent writers. His fictional narratives of rampant junkie abuse, county jail antics, and hell-raising in Southern Cal often made our hair stand on end. A question popped up from Gene H: "Does Criminal Class Press feature just prison writings?"

"Not at all," said Kent. "Oddly enough, it's just the name of the publication. They have a Web site, www.criminalclasspress.com, where people can buy all of their journals. They even sell their stuff in Europe, specifically in Paris.

"Picture a tall, beautiful Frenchwoman sitting in a posh café in Paris sipping a cappuccino and reading *your* stuff."

"OOOOoooohhhhh!!" The room erupted in gasps. With so much testosterone percolating, such an image was almost too much to bear.

On March 4, 2011, ten MFA (Masters of Fine Arts) graduate students with art and literature degrees from the California College of the Arts (CCA) in San Francisco showed up at the East Gate to take on our H-Unit scribes for Throwdown #2. When we'd first met this daring bunch of talented young male and female writers, we knew there was *no way in hell* that we could have demonstrated that kind of maturity back when we were earning our Bachelor of Arts degrees at San Francisco State University.

Anne Marino, one of the published writers who'd competed in the first Throwdown and a literary instructor at CCA, had received permission from the college to teach a graduate creative writing course called "Slammer: Writing In and About Prison." We stopped by her class to meet and speak with the students about H-Unit, and to describe our weekly routine as hired gun writers. Anne's idea was to bring her students into San Quentin to compete in the same Throwdown she had participated in. Her college department was very keen on the idea, since it dovetailed nicely with the current trend in colleges and universities to enlighten students beyond the classroom by letting them experience unique educational happenings outside their classrooms in the real world.

We applauded the concept. Our wily students qualified as unique, and visiting the Q and seeing firsthand how America warehouses its inmates definitely qualified as "real world."

Bringing an outside entourage into a lockdown facility isn't easy. One never knows if the daily routines of head count and chow will be on schedule. There's always the possibility of being turned away after a sudden lockdown, often predicated on spontaneous incidents of violence and reprisals, which can occur anywhere in the prison. Luckily, our guests at the gate once again conformed to the civilian dress code: no blue, denim, orange, or green attire. Plus, everybody had worn shoes that they could run in! While ID's are being checked and gate pass entries processed, one snag can mess up the whole process, so we were pleased that our guests had come as prepared to follow protocol as possible.

Like our previous group of visiting authors, the CCA student crew received preliminary instructions from the officer stationed at the main gate, and from Laura Bowman-Salzsieder, the Community Partnerships Manager who continually watched our backs. Laura helped escort our wide-eyed visiting party through two more sign-ins, metal detector security, and out onto the H-Unit yard itself on an especially bleak, overcast, and windy spring night.

Six thirty-five P.M. The overall mood on the yard seemed more ominous and tense than usual. It's funny how a prison yard can throw out that vibe of uncertainty. We'd often noticed a certain tension in the atmosphere when groups from each race huddled together, or as inmates stationed themselves at certain corners, standing uncharacteristically silent and watchful. It's an eerie feeling that CO's live with constantly.

This time the dorms had a CO dressed in khaki camouflage garb posted in front of each doorway. One held a rubber bullet riot weapon slung over his shoulder. We were relieved to find out that chow had already finished on time and that all we were waiting for was knife clearance from the kitchen detail. We joked with our visitors to loosen them up as they took in the sobering sights of prison for the first time. Being detained for a few hours, surrounded by bales of swirling razor wire atop high fences, and patrolled by gun towers at each corner, would be a memorable experience in their collegiate careers.

Unlike at the first competition, our defending champs entered the classroom minus their game faces. Greg C., our resident class poet, who bared an uncanny resemblance to Cosmo Kramer on the *Seinfeld* TV show, including the character's ADHD quirkiness, greeted the visiting students with a short, welcoming piece that ended with a good-natured but well-placed jab.

"Youse guys are in trouble," he said with a wide smile. "And just so you know, trouble was the only thing we were good at."

Unlike the published authors during Throwdown #1, this group of visitors was rather foolhardy. Max, one of the dozen students scattered around the room, responded to Carter's jab by proclaiming impending victory. The guys appreciated the visiting writers' cockiness. Their youthful enthusiasm was contagious and cut through the dire vibes that had emitted from the yard when we'd first arrived.

For Throwdown #2 we threw out a simpler writing topic. Three words were scrawled up on the dry board: AT THE CROSSROADS. Like any good writing topic, it was a subject the contestants could take literally or philosophically. Completion time was thirty minutes. Ready, aim, write!

In reading back the finished writings the following week— eight entries per side—we again found it surprisingly difficult to ascertain which side was which. We read tales of robbery, assault, clipped dialogue between a couple over adultery, and the devil himself meeting bluesman Robert Johnson at the crossroads— and these pieces were authored by the MFA grads! The H-Unit gang responded with dexterous narratives of hashish deals in the alleys of Calcutta, GBH (gross bodily harm) in a skid row motel, and a drunken car crash in frigid waters, Teddy Kennedy-Chappaquiddick style.

During the competition's ReadBack, scoring between the competing sides stayed fairly close until the three judges (two authors and an academic from CCA) heard a short but powerful time line piece written by H-Unit's James B.:

1986. (Four years old.) Momma! Why you burnin' that spoon with a lighter? You sick, momma? Why you giving yourself a shot?

1990. Mom, there's a whole bunch of police outside. Mom, why are they taking me? I didn't do anything wrong. I don't want to go.

1992. Mom, when can I come home? What do you mean I have to wait 'til you pass a drug class? How long does that take? Six months, that's all, and then I can come home? You promise?

2000. Mom, I hate you! You promised that you would come get me. All this over a drug? I can't believe you would abandon your own flesh and blood just because you can't stop getting high. I'll never be like you. I'll never leave my kid!

2008. Hey Honey! Daddy misses you. I only have two more years to go. Then I'll be home. I know I promised I would never leave you. I just made a mistake. I promise it will never happen again.

When I came to the crossroads, I had a choice to follow the map my mom drew for me or make that turn and take the right path. I chose the wrong way. Now I'm doing the same thing to my daughter that my mother did to me. Is it too late to make a U-turn? Maybe I can find a shortcut. I just pray I don't get lost on the way back.

James B.'s entry earned high scores across the board. When the final tabulations came through, the H-Unit writers handily defeated the MFA posse 298 to 227. Although the SQ knuckleheads were victorious once again, the hero—or rather heroine—of the event was Rachel from the CCA crew. Rachel had penned a particularly feisty tale of two females trapped in the hot sun with a broken-down auto. The story ended with one woman fatally clobbering the other across the head with an empty gas can before help arrived. The inmates were impressed with the snappiness and toughness of her story and its unexpected violent ending.

As important as our SQ class was, we still needed to earn a living. So we spent the week after Throwdown #2 in Chicago promoting *Operation Family Secrets*. Frank Calabrese, Jr. appeared on ABC's *Nightline*, followed by an expanded interview on NPR's *Fresh Air*. Since Calabrese had dodged the media over the past decade during the high-profile trials, he was in high demand in and around the Windy City. We had cameos on four major TV news outlets (ABC/CBS/NBC/FOX), plus radio spots with Greg Jarrett on WGN and Richard Roeper on WLS, and an exclusive print interview with press icon John Kass of the *Chicago Tribune*. We followed those appearances with a solid PBS television appearance on WTTW's *Chicago Tonight* and ended the weeklong agenda by joining Calabrese onstage for a presentation, discussion, and book signing with the esteemed Union League of Chicago.

A series of signings at Borders bookstores was abruptly cancelled when the chain received a threatening phone message. While we took the news in relative stride by hiring a bodyguard, the telephoned threat only succeeded in igniting a second firestorm of media interviews across the city. Once we returned from the tour, we received an urgent e-mail message from our literary agent, which we announced to the class that Friday.

"We just heard from our agent and editor that *Operation Family Secrets* debuted on the *New York Times* bestseller list at Number Fourteen."

The notoriety of the Chicago press following the threats, combined with the coast-to-coast reach of *Fresh Air* and *Nightline,* was enough to push us over the top and gain us our third bestseller. We were chuffed, but there was little time to celebrate or reflect. It was time to ramp up the next few projects.

After nearly a month of delays, the bound copies of Criminal Class Press Vol. 4 No. 2 arrived at H-Unit in the summer of 2011. We had turned in 55,000 words of classroom prose written between October 2010 and March 2011. Criminal Class Press had enlisted the services of artist Tony Fitzpatrick to provide their first four-color cover, a splendid piece entitled "Star of the Eternal City." Fitzpatrick's folksy canvases had appeared in museums across the country, including the Guggenheim in New York City. Inside pop culture circles, his artwork is best known for appearing on several CD's by American singer/ songwriter Steve Earle. It was an appropriate choice, being that Earle had once done a hard stretch in jail on drug charges during the 1990s, and had rallied publicly against the death penalty.

The finished books were sent to the receiving warehouse at San Quentin with the proper paperwork filled out and attached in triplicate. One false move and the entire shipment could have been rejected and sent back to Chicago. Because of the ongoing problem with illicit tobacco, drugs, cell phone smuggling, and other forms of contraband, every parcel that crossed the East Gate had to be scrutinized down to each individual piece.

Three weeks came and went and still no books in class, as they sat stranded in the warehouse. Each time the CO's unlocked the classroom door and announced the class, we were greeted with the same query from each inmate.

"Books in yet?"

"Nope."

Tim the cynic lost hope. "I'm tellin' ya," he warned us, "we won't see 'em."

Finally, on July 22nd, Laura came down from the hill to help us distribute the copies. Each inmate received two copies to take back to their bunks—one to keep and another copy to send to family. We staged a mini-celebration as everyone signed each other's copies. Regulations prevented us from providing refreshments and finger food so, in lieu of wine and cheese, we read aloud the four-page introduction that we had written. The back cover listed the names of each and every contributor. Featured were our choice writing topics: My Space, What Truly Scares Me, My Click Moment, At the Crossroads, and our two perennial favorites, Tattoos & Scars, and Upon Arrival. One section featured the selected works of three writers, Joseph H., Earl B., and Dinero D the Dynamic "P." Sprinkled amidst the text were a dozen poems by Greg C. And as promised, each class member had become a published writer. We'd kept our promise, and Tim the cynic was proven wrong once again.

By the fall of 2011 we had reached another milestone: we were drawing nearly 40 students per week. Plus, the students were 2-0 in their Throwdowns. As writers and teachers, we were firing on all cylinders. Word counts soared. Regular assignments typed up for ReadBack passed the 9,000-word mark, up to 18 pages of single-spaced text. A visiting poet/novelist told us that he felt lucky if 25 percent of college students in a classroom were enthusiastic and paying attention. He felt the opposite vibe in our class: 90 percent tuned in. Each week, the room was wired. H-Unit writing had reached a fevered pitch and "Finding Your Voice on the Page" was bursting at the seams. With an energy level so high, we knew that soon something would bring things back down to a dull roar. That something came from a highly unlikely source: the Supreme Court of the United States.

CHAPTER 25

Realignment and Reestablishing Contact

By the end of 2011, California's 33 state prisons, housing up to 160,000 inmates, were ordered to undergo a spring cleaning. In late May of 2011, the United States Supreme Court ordered the state of California to buck up and deal with the issue of overcrowding by "reassigning" as many as 48,000 (or as few as 37,000) incarcerated inmates across the state prison system. Up until then, most California prisons had been operating at nearly *double* the original "design capacity"—fancy talk for the total number of useable beds per institution. After a lawsuit filed against the state in 1990 on behalf of prison inmates, the case had worked its way up to the big leagues. By May 23, 2011, the U.S. Supreme Court put the hammer down. The problem of prison overcrowding needed to be addressed.

Among the residual effects of overcrowding were 112 inmate deaths in California due to inadequate medical care during 2008 and 2009 alone. There were reports of instances of overcrowding that had resulted in men being held in cages, supply closets, and laundry rooms, and a suicide rate that had grown to over double the national average. California and eighteen other states, most notably Texas, Alaska, and South Carolina, had issues potentially related to prison overcrowding.

"These violations have persisted for years," U.S. Supreme Court Justice Anthony Kennedy, one of the five justices ruling in favor of inmate rights' attorneys, wrote. "And they remain uncorrected."

According to Justices Ruth Bader Ginsburg, Stephen Breyer, Sonia Sotomayor, Elena Kagan, and Kennedy, housing inmates at 190 percent of a prison's "design capacity" violated constitutional protections against cruel and unusual punishment.

Part of what pushed the five consenting justices into ruling in favor of the inmates' attorneys was an unprecedented slide show of stark black-and-white pictures showing dorms (not unlike H-Unit) with rows and rows of crowded bunks. Those pictures weren't enough to persuade the four dissenters, Justices Antonin Scalia, Samuel Alito, John Roberts, Jr., and Clarence Thomas, who opposed the ruling, warning of pending dire consequences. According to the minority opinion, such a "radical" decision would result in a "staggering number" of felons endangering the lives of innocent Californians.

"I fear that today's decision, like prior prisoner release orders, will lead to a grim roster of victims," said Justice Samuel Alito.

Donald Specter, director of the nonprofit Prison Law Office, countered Alito: "This landmark decision will . . . make the prisons safer for the staff, improve public safety, and save the taxpayers billions of dollars."

Without authorizing a specific plan that California had to follow, the court declared that a prisoner release plan was to be organized, with a three-judge panel overseeing steps to alleviate the problem of prison overpopulation while newly elected California Governor Jerry Brown immediately green-lit California's pathway towards compliance.

"I will take all steps necessary to protect public safety," Governor Jerry Brown said, adding that "full and constitutionally guaranteed funding" for state and county programs was necessary to solve the problem.

As a direct result, California passed Assembly Bills 109 and 117, among other measures, outlining the state's course of action. AB 109 would specifically become "the cornerstone of California's solution for reducing the number of inmates in the state's 33 institutions." Specifically, the CDCR needed to trim California's prison capacity down to approximately 137.5 percent of "design capacity," or a statewide total of 110,000 inmates, by mid-2012. The 137.5 percent capacity number would be based on the average capacity of all 33 institutions.

By late November and early December of 2011, the CDCR acted and the face of San Quentin was immediately altered. Most notable was the elimination of West Block as a "reception center." No longer would San Quentin be a distribution point, dispensing and circulating newly arrived inmates throughout the various state institutions. No longer would orange jumpsuited arrivals be housed in makeshift places like the prison gymnasium for months. Rather, West Block would once again be used to house existing full-time inmates while San Quentin's population would be reduced by about a thousand inmates to just over four thousand total.

Contrary to widespread misconception, California's realignment plan didn't include kicking state prison inmates down to county jails. Nor would the state prematurely release anyone. Instead, newly convicted inmates, particularly the "three nons" (nonviolent, nonsexual, nonserious felons), would no longer be automatically shipped off to a California State Prison. Lesser institutions like treatment programs and county jails would take up the slack, which would require additional state funding. Judges would be more mindful in sentencing. More authority would be placed on street-level parole authorities, who are believed to be more attuned to the realities of reentry. As a result, California's prison landscape would soon change significantly.

By June 2010, California no longer had the highest population of state prison inmates. California, whose state prison facilities had topped 173,000 in 2006, now had fewer than 136,000 state convicts. Texas, with its 154,000 prisoners, took over first place, and Florida landed third place with about 100,000 in lockdown.

Those of us inside the STAND UP program in H-Unit immediately felt the jolt of change. Rather than paperwork, statistics, and percentages, we were dealing with human beings with names and faces. Coincidentally, at the time, our class was overcrowded to the degree that we were beginning to get complaints from the longer term students who felt that the growing number attending was making the class somewhat unwieldy. We agreed. The average ReadBack now took two entire class sessions, cutting our writing time in half. Plus, just typing up the stories during the week took about ten combined hours, not counting class prep time.

Realignment put a quick end to all of that.

In October the first batch of H-Unit inmates were reassigned to West Block. We lost six of our best students, including Tim the cynic, Frenchie, and Raul. While H-Unit students could walk up the hill to the Small Yard to take open university classes (if they weren't already filled up), those reassigned uphill to West or North Block with more stringent security procedures couldn't walk down to H-Unit to partake in the STAND UP program, where we were headquartered. According to the gossip on the grapevine, the West Block cells were dank and decrepit. Over the years, the incoming new guys from Reception had done a number on the place. Plugs and light sockets were trashed. Cells lacked electricity. Extension cords ran everywhere. We felt sad for our lost exiled brothers. We especially missed Tim's skeptical responses from the back of the classroom.

After watching some of our STAND UP students being shipped out, a few of the more vocal teachers whose classes had been gutted due to reassignments spoke up. They proposed to the H-Unit custody staff CO's that rather than ship out inmates who were "programming" or had jobs, why not start with those not taking classes or working? After a meeting with a core of STAND UP teachers along with the assistant warden and a few of the H-Unit CO's, an informal agreement was struck that an attempt would be made to limit the shipping out of inmates who were gainfully employed or were programming. We pushed for the remote possibility that one day H-Unit could exclusively house those inmates embracing not only rehabilitation, but education and self-improvement. An entire yard devoted entirely to men with jobs and those taking classes! Education du jour!

Once again, "Finding Your Voice on the Page" survived the hurricane winds of change, which this time had arrived via an edict from the higher-ups on the federal and state levels. While we'd lost a few key students, once the reassignment smoke cleared, we were left with a more manageable class size. A new era of growth and development for the class was coming. Who knew what might transpire?

As a result, since less serious offenders might not reach the state prison level, we began teaching a harder-edged brand of career inmates, which was fine with us. We'd found that writing talent surfaces across the entire behavioral spectrum. To paraphrase the old saying, writing "soothes the savage beast"—whether we are dealing with drug offenders, parole violators, or felons guilty of more serious and violent offenses, we don't care. Good writing emanates from good writers, regardless of their crimes and foibles. Our mission continues: demystify the art and craft of writing to the degree that practically anybody can partake. Who better to debunk that myth than a classroom full of San Quentin Sweathog jailbirds!

Justice is a funny thing, particularly when viewing the end results from a front-row seat. While not one Catholic bishop or too-big-to-fail banker in our country has done time for their crimes against children or America's 2007 and 2008 economic near-collapse, we've watched the Average Joes, mostly comprised of the poor and working class, systematically do maximum, iron-fisted time for their infractions against society. Bob Dylan was right when he said, "steal a little and they throw you in jail, steal a lot and they make you king."

CHAPTER 26

The Ballad of Big Bob

Amidst the matters of state politics, court orders, and realignment, on a more personal level, we reestablished contact with Big Bob. When we last left Big Bob—dubbed by the local media as "the Broken Nose Bandit"—he was mired in a litany of pre-sentencing appearances for his bank robberies. Just to refresh your memory, once upon a time Big Bob had been a confident San Quentin alumnus. Then, like a lot of small business owners, his world had caved in when his credit lines dried up and his loans were called in by the big banks in 2008. Big Bob, already in way over his head, fell high and hard, fueled by depression, drug abuse, and desperation.

In October 2011, a mutual friend had forwarded a letter from Bob that answered a lot of questions about his ultimate fate. Big Bob was still a colorful symbol to us, a real-life character who even inspired a fictional one in one of our pulp novels, *6 Chambers, 1 Bullet*. Bob reminded us of the frailty of the American Dream and the frontier tradition of success at all costs. As life in the USA becomes more and more of a huge gulf between the have's and the have-not's, it's painfully obvious that maintaining a working middle-class existence is more difficult than ever. If nothing else, Big Bob was testimony to that.

On September 22, 2011, Big Bob was sentenced to two 25-to-life terms for the 2008 robbery of a Wells Fargo bank. With two burglary strikes already on his past record, Bob's third-strike binge of robberies succeeded in getting him put away indefinitely. If two 25-to-life sentences sound excessive, it's a far cry from the original 705 years he'd accumulated by robbing 11 banks in 12 days, netting $176,000 before getting nabbed in a 7-Eleven parking lot. Yet to us, Big Bob will always be the guy who saved our asses in the lieutenant's office.

We sent him a letter in October 2011, and received an instant response. We pictured Big Bob's puckish smile wedged between the lines of the yellow legal-sized paper filled with his cursive scrawl.

"So what happened to Big Bob?" he wrote, answering a question we'd purposely avoided asking. "Well, let me say, it was like a 'Perfect Storm.' It was my fault, I accept the blame."

"My third day in [county] jail, I was facing 626-years-to-life under the Three Strikes Law, so I jumped off the second tier. I knocked myself unconscious and got to a hospital. While I was there, I took a cop's gun and tried to shoot myself. I was then charged with taking a police officer's weapon, attempting escape by force, and delaying an officer in his official duties. That put me up to 705-years-to-life."

"Let me say," Bob wrote us, "'I'm sorry,' to you both. I let you down. I broke the trust of our friendship by not reaching out to you before I did this. I should have let you both know that I needed help.

"As of today, well, I've never seen a prison like this one [North Kern County State Prison in Delano, California]," he went on, "and I've been in eight different ones in California. This place has a violent incident in my little cell block nearly every other day. It's just plain wild with lots of gang stuff, lots of attacks, two- or three-on-one person usually. You've got to keep your eyes (and ears) open.

"Don't misunderstand me. What I did was wrong. I'm sure those two women bank tellers will never forget that crazed look I had, all cracked out, handing them a note asking for the money in their teller drawers.

"I feel a lot of shame and guilt," Big Bob continued. "I look at the men around me and realize most of them didn't stand a chance in life. Me, well I was at least smart enough to make lemonade when I got lemons. I went to GED, then college, transferred my units, and got my BS in Environmental Studies.

"Have I given up? No, not as of yet. Hope I never do. But hearing the judge say 'life,' really was so shocking, with the courtroom nearly empty, just me, my lawyer, the DA, cops, and judge. Very painful."

At night, in the comfort of our own homes, we often wondered about Big Bob, as our disappointment in him turned to perplexity. How would Big Bob survive in that hostile new environment? We still recalled his childlike behavior at the NBA game shortly after his release. His is a vulnerability that we often see in other inmates, whether it's staged or genuine. What becomes of the brokenhearted? The answer is that many of them end up in San Quentin and countless other institutions, doing much more time than they'd imagined they would. Even under the influence of drugs, what the hell was Bob thinking? Could life have been that insurmountable?

"You guys, don't worry about Big Bob. With 20 years in the CDCR, I know how to jail. I think, honestly, that is why I broke bad. Pressure, bills, financials, being a dad, in my subconscious, this was the easy way out. I'm told when to eat, crap, and shower. Not a whole lot of decisions."

I spent 65 months living in San Quentin's H-Unit. During that time, there were many memories both good and bad. To say what my favorite memory is would be difficult. I could cheat and tell you about the day I paroled and rode the Larkspur ferry past H-Unit while flipping the bird with both hands at the H-Unit sally port tower guard. But that wouldn't be fair, because technically I was no longer "in" H-Unit.

I could tell you about the Friday night when the Z-men spent several hundred bucks on cake and ice cream for the entire Success Program dorm. While waiting to get into the chow hall, I was standing with the Z-men and someone lit a "stick." Keith turns to me and says, "I smell marijuana," and looked at me like he couldn't believe someone had a joint in H-Unit. The look on his face was priceless.

But my favorite H-Unit memory would be the day Metallica played at San Quentin. It was May 2003 and they were shooting a video in North Block for their St. Anger album. All day long at work, behind the 8 Wall, we could hear them blasting that song over and over. Then, the next day, they gave a concert on the Big Yard. The only H-Unit inmates allowed to go were the Success dorm students (now STAND UP).

About 50 of us went up there. It was a beautiful warm evening, like about 5 P.M., right after count cleared. It was crowded, but I got a spot about 15 feet from the stage. It was James Trujillo's first gig on bass with the band. James Hetfield had just gotten out of rehab (two weeks before) and had cut his long hair. Lars Ulrich and Kirk Hammett were off the hook. They played 16 songs that night. It was like I wasn't in prison for three hours. I will never forget that night and will always "hold up" Metallica for coming into that hellhole San Quentin and giving us that show. That is my favorite memory from my time in H-Unit.

—Big Bob

EPILOGUE

Statistics Are . . .

An American scientist named Dr. Irving Selikoff, known for having discovered the harmful link between lung ailments and breathing asbestos particles, said it best:

"Statistics are people with the tears wiped away."

By that we think he means that once you humanize a situation and attach a name, face, and life story to it, your outlook on a man or woman changes. Suppose you're a strict evangelical Christian and you're strongly opposed to gay marriage. Then a gay couple moves across the street from you and they're the best neighbors you've ever had. You make friends with them, and suddenly the scepter of gay rights isn't so ominous.

The same thing applies to working with men in prison. On the surface, incarcerated felons are hardened statistics. Society has ostracized them so we don't deal with them in our everyday lives, which is understandable. But when we get to interact with each other as individuals and not as two separate social groups, the walls (pardon the pun) inevitably come down. And that's the value of volunteerism.

In reading the hundreds of thousands of words from the men who have enrolled over the years in "Finding Your Voice on the

Page" and bared their souls, the three most dominant emotions portrayed in their writings are: Remorse, Defiance, and Regret. The Q has taught us the amplified power of those feelings, and as often as these men express raw insubordination and rage, many of them—to quote Leonard Cohen—"never lament casually" over their mistakes and shortcomings.

Prison has seeped into our lives in this country as entertainment. We are fascinated by crime and punishment. It's like driving by a car wreck. We need to look. But at the same time, we've opened Pandora's Box by throwing it up on the television screen. We now know what goes on. No more "out of sight, out of mind." Forbidden and hideous places like the Hole, solitary confinement, and Level 4 lockdowns are beamed into our living rooms.

We two have learned a few central truths on our journey behind the walls and razor wire. First off, being around prisons and fraternizing with guys who are assigned five-digit numbers with a big yellow "CDCR" plastered on their backs makes you instantly realize how sacred basic creature comforts are. Oh, how sweet it is to take a bath and then get up, turn on the basketball game, do a load of laundry, and grill yourself a big ol' cheese sandwich. Heaven!

For almost a decade every Friday, we've been surrounded by guys who we playfully call "the Knuckleheads," i.e., incarcerated dudes who often lack life's most basic management skills. In this day and age of high stakes, high tech, high economic volatility, and ever-changing situational morality, having command of basic life management skills has never been more important.

Lou Reed once wrote, "there is no time," and he's right. There is no time in the modern age to screw up. There is no time to become an alcoholic. There is no time to carry a drug monkey on your back and become a junkie, dope fiend, cokehead, pothead, tweaker, or whatever the polite term is for an addict. There is no time to be a scammer and commit crimes. There is no time to screw everything that moves and have illegitimate babies. There is no time to get pulled over for drunk driving. There is no time to rough up your spouse and attract the cops, because when you do these things, you risk getting stuck in the revolving door of corrections, which reduces you to second-class citizenry.

So to the "everyday people," which includes us—*you* are today's heroes on these mean streets of America. Dear reader, don't underestimate your seemingly mundane but vitally important life management skills like: 1) running a business; 2) maintaining a marriage or domestic partnership; 3) raising children and a family; and 4) keeping your head above water financially. The gilded rich and privileged might think otherwise, but like baseball star Reggie Jackson once said, "We are the straw that stirs the drink" in this society.

Another universal life lesson we've learned behind San Quentin's walls is that our past never escapes us. It's like a creeping shadow. The past will always haunt you. Working with people in prison has made us question everything about living in a so-called democratic society. Visiting prison as outsiders has forced us to reassess our attitudes about certain absolutes in our ordered social system—traditional bastions like law, morality, sobriety, enforcement, religion, capitalism, justice, and our local, state, and federal political structures.

The most troubling social trend since we started our work in San Quentin has been the rise of corporatism. Corporatism rules our society. Money buys power and perverts justice. It controls the hallways of our assemblies, parliaments, legislatures, and courtrooms. Corporatism touches everything, including prisons. Decades ago, it would have been inconceivable for custody and corrections to be taken over by private companies publicly traded on the stock market. Privatized prisons? It's come to this.

It's a tired cliché, but it's true: Prison is a microcosm. Just as our inmates can't get out of their own way, the apparatus of our criminal justice system can become so cumbersome: it can't get out of its own way, either, no matter how good its intentions are. At the same time, while our prison systems can become as dysfunctional and corrupt as the inmates they house, and while it's fashionable to criticize and demonize government services, most of the people we've met working inside the public sector are the thin blue line between our liberty and anarchy. And we salute them. Even the inmates, when pressed, will admit that prison isn't merely a story of black hats and white hats, but rather one of a wide spectrum of gray hats trying to do their best given the tools they have to work with.

When we voluntarily entered into this unusual subculture we found that what Joe had said at the dinner table that day was true. Men can change given the right tools. So many of our students have experienced such horrendous and abusive lives (often of their own making) that simple compassion or a keen interest in hearing their stories can trigger a Click Moment inside their psyches which can help them turn their lives around.

Although we still don't consider ourselves as "hug-a-thugs," our main role behind the walls can be neatly explained by a line from the motion picture, *The King's Speech,* in which Lionel Logue, the film's protagonist, who served as speech therapist to King George VI, explains, "My job is to give them faith in their own voice and let them know that a friend was listening."

Recalling the days when Bobby Lee sat by the door of the classroom taking it all in before his untimely death, well, at least he knew two things: we were listening, and we were friends.

Education is just as important as listening. In fact, education is God, and God is education. We can't get enough. You can't OD on education. Education is still our number one social commodity, hands down. Most of the problems in our society can be solved through education via schools, colleges, universities, vocational and career training, community centers, prisons, detention facilities, day care centers, detox wards, mental institutions, and wayward shelters. Through education, we could forestall so much crime, addiction, affliction, illiteracy, ignorance, hatred, poverty, and suffering through a stimulus that would pay off and leave us with an informed populace and a more learned and sophisticated workforce.

And finally, dear reader, Viva Volunteerism! Take the plunge and pitch in! Help our society with whatever skills you have to offer that will help others get back on their feet again. And in the case of prisons and jails, do it without getting sucked into the dark side. Respect the line between good and evil, and be careful not to cross it.

In 2011 we made the decision to obtain nonprofit status for "Finding Your Voice on the Page," with the hopes of possibly expanding it sometime in the future. Gaining 501(c)(3) nonprofit status was a completely and utterly daunting process. Standing between any organization large or small and nonprofit status is mountains of paperwork, potential legal and accounting fees, and state and federal qualifications that must be met.

We got lucky on two fronts. After 20-plus years, we reestablished a connection with a long-lost friend named Paul McNabb, who works in the world of fundraising, grant application, and nonprofit organizations. Combined with our good karma, Paul led us in the right direction and gave us the necessary confidence to venture down the nonprofit road.

We later found out that achieving nonprofit status could be done far more easily than we'd first thought, thanks to a fine organization in San Francisco called Intersection for the Arts. After a few persuasive sit-downs with their screening personnel, we were accepted into their organization. Intersection then brought us into their incubator program, and took us under their wing to use their nonprofit status in soliciting grants and funds. For a reasonable percentage fee, they manage and distribute whatever funds budding organizations raise. So far, it's been the perfect vehicle to allow us to do our thing and not be saddled with cumbersome nonprofit legal and accounting burdens. Rather than apply for our individual nonprofit status in the early stages, IFTA enabled us to piggyback onto their status during our formative developing years.

In 2010 the Yardtime Literary Project (YLP) was born and was sanctioned as a legitimate nonprofit entity. As a result we have attracted modest funds to keep our San Quentin class functioning. But wouldn't it be something if we could branch out and create more writing programs that would help other poor and underserved people find their voices on the page?

Through the YLP, our long-term goal is to one day expand and raise money to replicate our class at other institutions, and possibly hire other local writers from around the area. After that, we have a dream: What if we could expand our "Finding Your Voice on the Page" classroom concepts and share them with the Bay Area community in general? What if the YLP could use our ReadBack writing and teaching methods in, again, places like elderly folks' homes, battered-women's shelters, and other local community centers? One of our long-term goals as teachers is to expand the class while maintaining a firm base of support for the STAND UP class at San Quentin.

Getting the YLP to thrive beyond San Quentin is going to be a major endeavor. But it is one that we would seriously like to pursue one day, when the book-writing muse abandons us and we make our inevitable exit from the artistic and creative stage to community service . . . or, as Leonard Cohen once cryptically described it, "summoned now to deal with your invincible defeat."

Nonetheless, we'll carry on, no matter how long it takes.

So wish us and our Yardtime Literary Program the best of luck so that one day we can achieve our goals and move on to not only greener pastures, but more expansive ones.

APPENDIX

20 Questions from the Children

Lots of people, particularly satellite/cable television view-ers, are interested in the stories and the plight of the incarcerated. (Otherwise, we wouldn't have written this book.) Prison makes for excellent cocktail and dinner party chatter. It seems as if everyone has an opinion. We've encountered lots of curious folks. People are concerned from a humane and societal standpoint, or they are angry and frustrated that our culture warehouses and, as some see it, cod-dles criminals. It's only recently that the financial concerns, specifi-cally, are being voiced across the entire political spectrum.

Millions of TV viewers watch the popular cable prison shows, like MSNBC's *Lockdown* series, and the various unscripted docu-mentary shows on the Discovery and National Geographic chan-nels. Most of these shows are told primarily through the lens of law enforcement and display the grisly side of prison. They feature spooky, deranged inmates with neck tats, missing teeth, and limited inbred intelligence. People we've met who work in television often refer to these shows as "prison porn."

Besides the questions we routinely get at cocktail and dinner parties, the most interesting queries of all came from a class of ten- and eleven-year-olds attending school in Brooklyn where a former music business associate of ours teaches. We received an e-mail request from her out of the blue.

> Kent and Keith: Would it be possible for my students to send you a few questions to answer about your experiences as a prison reformer? I know you and Keith teach writing to inmates at San Quentin State Prison and I think the work you do would be very valuable to my students. Please let me know if we can send you questions.

Two things struck us in reading this letter. First, we'd never been described as "prison reformers" before, which we found amusing and dear. Second, we were fascinated by the idea of what questions ten- or eleven-year-olds might have about prison, considering the imagery they are bombarded with from movies, television, video games, and online content. Children have a way of getting to the heart of any matter. Here are their questions, followed by our candid responses.

1. Has a prisoner ever written a gory sentence?

Good question, because most of our writing is done in the classroom in short, spontaneous 30-40 minute bursts. It's like: ready, set, write! When we teach writing, we stress that, whenever possible, a writer should draw on firsthand knowledge. As a result, the men in our writing class generally write from their life experiences. Their stories can be quite rambunctious. They might range from high-speed car chases to their thoughts about being locked up, to who and what they miss most on the outside. The subjects can range from the simplest (your favorite car or pet) to things deeper, regarding their feelings about family as well as love and fear and other things we all have in common. But to answer your question, we can recall one inmate's writing that was especially gory (and incriminating) in which he wrote about protecting his family against someone whom he considered dangerous. In the piece, he wrote about his own act of violence involving a gun and some poor guy's face being shot off. Of course, we were concerned about typing up the story, photocopying it, and passing it around to the class. So we omitted the most violent part, to which the inmate later responded, "That's all right. You could have left it in. I did the time for that one."

2. Has there ever been violence in your class?

At H-Unit inside San Quentin State Prison, the classroom is regarded as a violence-free zone. It's like a church; if an inmate is trying to better himself, the classroom is a sanctuary of sorts, and violence is off-limits. That said, besides some across-the-room bantering by some of the guys, we've only come close to physical violence once in our classroom when a fight nearly broke out between two rather tough guys. One was a guy who was doing time for accidentally killing another guy in a bar fight. Up to that time, he was rather even-tempered. The other guy was a big tough dude who happened to be openly gay. He was one of the rowdiest guys in our classroom, quite aggressive and in-your-face. When the two guys jumped out of their chairs and assumed their fighting positions to square off, Kent ran to the back of the room where the fight was brewing while Keith stationed himself at the front door. Nothing further happened. Since we're unarmed, we are required to wear whistles. If any violence breaks out, we're instructed to blow our whistles three times—the international signal for distress—and help is on the way. By the way, the "watch station" where the officers work is right next door to our classroom so, while we're careful, we're not afraid.

3. Do you think prisoners can change?

Yes. We want to believe people can change, though they don't always. We've been disappointed by guys who were released and immediately reverted back to the same criminal behavior that got them in prison in the first place. Whenever a student comes up to us and says he's being released, we ask him the same question. Are you done? Meaning, are you finished going back and forth to prison? Are you through disappointing your family, your children, and your loved ones? Usually the answer is yes, though statistically, 67 percent of the people in California who leave jail come back. It's called recidivism. But the best answer to your question came from a guy who was a San Quentin warden. His name was Clinton Duffy. He wrote a few books about prison, one of which we read when we were about your age. He opposed the death penalty. He eliminated racial segregation and corporal punishment, pushed for better food, started the San Quentin newspaper, and brought Alcoholics Anonymous into the prison. Warden Duffy, a true prison reformer, was an extremely progressive man who believed in rehabilitation at a time when most everyone else in the country believed in severe punishment. A critic of Warden Clinton Duffy once said to him, "Don't you know that leopards can't change their spots?" To which he responded, "You should know that I don't work with leopards. I work with men, and men change every day."

4. Do you think the prisoners write after they are released?

We know they do. We've kept in touch with a few of the men, and yes, some keep writing. Some become involved in other areas of the arts as a result of our class. We've known some who have become actors in local plays. We say, when you get out of prison, take a class instead of hanging out on the streets. For every class a former inmate takes, there's less of a chance he'll come back to prison. Writing is a good way for a person to look inside themselves and realize what it is they're doing wrong and what it is they're doing right. Looking at your life as a story gives you a different perspective.

5. What makes you feel safe around the prisoners?

While we try to maintain a professional distance between the men and ourselves, particularly not revealing too much of our private lives, it's like when we wrote books with bikers or mobsters. Being in a classroom with 30 prisoners who appreciate you coming in each week to teach the class and to help them learn and occupy their time is like being in a room with 30 bodyguards. We're the most protected two guys in the whole prison. That said, we try not to be too casual about safety. We constantly pay attention to what's going on in the room.

6. Do you teach anything else except writing?

Maybe a little poetry or screenwriting, though we're not experts in either field. We think that by teaching the men about writing and finding their voices on the page, we're teaching them how to examine their thoughts and improve their character. We talk a lot about the publishing business. We try to maintain a vocational aspect to our teaching, as in how to possibly make a living as a writer. Since the men have no computers, we try to describe the latest technology so that when they get out, they're vaguely familiar with what's going on. We talk about what's happening in the world. A lot of times, that's where we find our subjects to assign for the men to write about.

7. Do your prison students have homework? If they do, do they like doing it?

We rarely assign homework, though whenever we do, it's because the men specifically ask for it. Our writing assignments tend to be like pop quizzes. Rather than just write an assignment that's sprung on them that day in class, occasionally the guys like to know what they'll be writing about the following week so they can come to class better prepared, or else they might want to find some time during the week to do some writing before our Friday night class starts. But our students don't live in cells. They live in large dormitories that are loud and noisy, making it difficult to concentrate and do homework. That's why most of the writing is done in-class.

8. Why did you choose to be a prison reformer?

As young kids we read a library book by Warden Clinton Duffy called *88 Men and 2 Women*. It was about the death penalty and it was written in 1962. But our biggest influence came from two men: our father, Joseph Zimmerman, and Johnny Cash, the country singer and legend. Our father, Joe, once went to San Quentin and was so struck by his visit he wanted to teach a class on salesmanship. He didn't get to do it, so we're fulfilling the dream. As kids, we were raised to believe that people are people, whether they're rich or poor, free or in jail. Johnny Cash was famous for performing live in prisons for the inmates. He related to the men on three levels, from his head, his heart, and his gut. There's not a time when we go to prison that we don't think about Johnny. He taught us how to relate to tough guys in prison, not by trying to be tough like them, but by "keeping it real." Our students aren't looking for tough guys. They see tough guys all week. They're looking for people who keep it real and don't talk down to them.

9. Have you ever made friends with the prisoners?

Yes, and it's risky in that people can impress you inside, but disappoint you outside. One guy we made friends with ended up robbing a bunch of banks after he got out. That shook our faith in what we were doing. However, we've kept in touch with a handful of men who, like everyone else, are struggling to survive in a tough economy, in a country where corporations and rich people hold most of the cards. But we persevere and press onward! For some odd reason, we've written a lot of books with people who have been in prison. Don't ask us why, since we've never been arrested or thrown in jail, knock on wood.

10. Were you scared at first?

The first time we went inside San Quentin State Prison to meet the person in charge of education, we weren't scared so much as we were fascinated and anxious to see what it was about San Quentin that had inspired our father, Joe, and our mentor, Johnny Cash. The first time we stood up to teach our class, we were terrified, not necessarily scared of being harmed, more nervous, like when you speak in front of the class. You overcome your fears. Every time we go inside, we're a tiny bit nervous and scared. We've been told that's a good thing—it keeps you on your toes. You don't want to be too comfortable or careless inside a prison.

11. What kind of topics do your prisoners write about?

We have them write about a bunch of subjects. Our favorite one is Tattoos & Scars. The guys write about the tattoos on their arms and bodies and where they came from. They write about their scars (or bullet holes) and where they got them, though sometimes they write about mental scars, things that happened to them when they were kids. Also, whenever we ask the men to write about animals and pets, we get some great pieces. Animals seem to bring out the best in people. Lots of people remember a certain dog, cat, or other pet or animal that touched their lives. One subject we like to assign is an inmate's favorite toy when they were kids. As we type up the assignments, we Google the names of the toys and pop in pictures alongside the writing. That blows their minds, seeing something from their childhoods that they haven't seen in years.

12. Do you like your job?

Yes. It's hard to make a living as a writer in the twenty-first century, let alone run a writing business that supports twin brothers. That's when we wish we owned and operated a delicatessen. But we like meeting and working with interesting people, except we don't recommend to kids like you that you become writers. Excel in math, science, and computer classes, then become a writer later.

13. Have you guys ever played baseball with the prisoners?

No, but we've watched a few games. There's a field inside the prison, not far from our classroom. We had one student named Herman who played infield for the San Quentin Giants. The team is sponsored by the San Francisco Giants, who help supply them with uniforms and equipment. The team has a coach and they play local amateur and semiprofessional teams. We remember watching one of their pitchers, tall and gangly, who looked exactly like the famous Major League pitcher Randy Johnson, except this pitcher was in prison for hitting his wife hard with a baseball bat. Thanks to Herman, we have a couple of autographed San Quentin team baseballs!

14. Do most prisoners write on paper or on computers?

Our guys only write on paper, on tablets we buy at the office supply store. We use plastic pens with no metal that can be sharpened and used as a weapon. No doubt the ink in our pens are used for tattoos, which we have no control over. Our motto: keep it simple (and legal) when bringing things inside a prison. As for computers, you don't want guys in prison having access to computers and the Internet. That might provide too much temptation to commit crimes or screw up.

15. Do they have detention and if they do, what do they have to do?

Yes, which brings up a troubling aspect of prison. At San Quentin, detention is called Administration Segregation, or Ad Seg, or the Hole. If you get in a fight, or get written up for a serious crime or infraction, you get sent to the Hole, which is in a section of San Quentin called Carson. We've heard many horror stories about being sent to the Hole. First, it's extremely lonely. You're isolated for days, weeks, or months. The only time you see anyone else is when they walk by, on their way to their cell. You only get to shower every couple of days. You communicate by "fishing," that is, you attach a note to thread or fishing line (who knows where they get it?), and throw it to an adjacent cell. In the Hole, you only get to go outside of your cell to a cage for one hour. Guys go nuts. One guy we knew spent months in the Hole. To keep from going insane, he walked between the walls of his cell 171,000 times just for something to do. It's a difficult situation. What do you do with inmates who habitually break the rules? Yet is it inhumane to put a person in a cage for weeks or months on end? The scariest part of San Quentin is called the Adjustment Center. It's for guys who are incapable of living with other human beings. We've never been inside, though we've heard that just the vibes that emanate from that place are creepy and evil. Some of the guys inside the Adjustment Center were even transferred over from Death Row.

16. Why do you help prisoners?

Not very many in America care about people in prison. Americans assume that men and women in prison deserve to be isolated from the rest of society. And while that might be true in most cases, they still need education. Some have made serious mistakes in their lives for which they must pay a debt to society. It seems that in America, the poor get blamed for most of the problems in our society, and that the more money you have, the less likely it is that you may have to pay for *your* mistakes. If you have enough money, you can hire the best attorneys and often not go to jail. Some bankers, after having stolen billions, live in mansions, while some guys steal ten dollars and go to prison for months or even years. As long as that is happening in this country, the only way we can fight back is to offer programs and education that shows criminals that they can change or better themselves. It's our only weapon against crime. As government programs and spending for the poor, the old, and the disadvantaged are cut, somebody has got to jump in and help out the so-called dregs of our society. Isn't that what this guy Jesus talked about?

17. Do you have a favorite student?

Like most teachers, we have "teacher's pets." Guys who are good writers. Guys who have perfect attendance. Guys who take the class seriously. Guys with interesting life stories. Our favorite students come in all shapes, sizes, and colors. The good thing about our class is that inside the classroom, the races seem to get along. Two of our "favorite students" were both named Frenchie, both black dudes. Frenchie #1 was in our class for about four years. We watched his writing skills blossom. He became a great writer. He was a leader and was looked up to, particularly by the younger students. He told some cool stories and became extremely self-aware. We often wonder what became of him after he was released to his home in Southern California. Frenchie #2 reminded us of Chris Rock. He was hilarious. His handwriting was atrocious. On the surface, it looked like the scrawl of a child. But once we typed up his stories and read what was inside his brain aloud to the class, his stories came alive. The entire class laughed themselves silly. When Frenchie #2 got shipped out and transferred to another section of the prison, we immediately missed him. Another one of our past students, a 300-pound guy, wrote a beautiful peace that Kent ended up reading at our father's memorial service. He was one of our favorite student writers, very talented.

18. How do you teach prisoners to write?

We stumbled almost accidentally upon a unique method of teaching writing. Our claim is that we can teach *anyone* to write. The way our class works is, we talk a little bit about the craft of writing. We read examples of good writing. We talk about the business of publishing. We talk about the books we've written, how they got done. After that, we come up with a writing subject, write it on the board, and give the students about a half hour to put something on the page. At the end of the class, we collect the writing. During the week we type up the writing into a document called *Hard Time, Yard Time, Our Time*. What's included in the document is the stuff written that week. We photocopy the writing, pass out a copy to everybody in the class, and then the two of us read back the writing out loud while the room follows along. We call it the ReadBack method. We're very careful to read the stories back dramatically. Once people hear something they've written read back like that, they can hardly believe they wrote it. As a result they get more and more confident until they see themselves as writers. From there the sky is the limit. Once people feel good about themselves, they do their best work. Our dream is to make our teaching method available outside of prison and adapt it to other communities, especially poorer folks or old people who are lonely in old folks' homes.

19. Do the prisoners like to go to class?

We make a deal with our students. As long as we get something out of the class, we'll keep doing it. As long as they get something out of the class, they'll keep coming. It has to be a mutually beneficial thing. We're not out to save the world. Some guys tell us that our class gets them through the week, and that it makes the days and weeks pass by faster. We once got in trouble with the guards because as our students saw us walking down the road, they hung out at the classroom door instead of staying in their bunks waiting for the "all clear" call. That must mean they like the class. So we had to tell our guys to refrain from hanging out in front of the door until the class was called over the loudspeakers. Once the class is announced over the loudspeakers, we like to watch the students, dressed in blue, walk to the class from across the prison yard clutching their notebooks, tablets, and pens. It's a funny sight.

20. How did you get involved in teaching at San Quentin?

Since we wanted to learn how to teach, we called the prison and asked if they were interested in having us offer a writing course. Since we'd written books with ex-criminals, we weren't sure they'd let us in. But they did, and we've been going inside almost every week since. Originally, we wanted to get enough teaching experience to one day quit writing and go get jobs teaching in college. But nine years later, we're still teaching in prison and are still writing books. Funny where life takes you.

Our section of the prison is comprised only of students who have release dates, meaning they'll rejoin society. We first became involved in a program started by then-warden Jeanne Woodford originally called the Success Program, later changed to STAND UP. Warden Woodford was a lot like Warden Duffy. She opposes the death penalty and is now a prison reformer after leaving the state prison system. Most of the volunteers in the STAND UP program teach self-help courses and programs, like parenting, nutrition, nonviolent communication, anger management, and even gardening and yoga. They conduct 12-step fellowship programs for alcohol and drug abuse. We're proud to say that our class is among the most popular inside the prison. It's unconventional. We don't censor or delete, unless it's something distastefully violent that could endanger an inmate writers release. We let them write about anything they want. Sometimes we use bad language while teaching, which is something you shouldn't do.